MORE
GOOD OLD MAINE

All the best
to Brunswick!

Will Anderson

This book is very lovingly dedicated to my wife,
Catherine, who understood - so very often -
my need to "process" and put words down
while they were fresh in my mind. And who
was then a gentle but constructive reader.
Without you MORE GOOD OLD MAINE would
most likely be mired somewhere around
second base.
And home would be very far away.

101 PAST & PRESENT POP DELIGHTS

MORE
GOOD OLD MAINE

by Will Anderson

Will Anderson, Publisher
7 Bramhall Terrace
Portland, Maine 04103

Other Books by the Author
BEER, NEW ENGLAND (1988)
NEW ENGLAND ROADSIDE DELIGHTS (1989)
MID-ATLANTIC ROADSIDE DELIGHTS (1991)
WAS BASEBALL REALLY INVENTED IN MAINE? (1992)
GOOD OLD MAINE (1993)

Library of Congress Catalogue Card Number: 95-75481

Anderson, Will 1940-
1. Popular Culture   2. Maine

ISBN 0-9601056-7-0

Studio photography by A. & J. Commercial Photography, Lewiston, Maine
Typeset and printed by Spectrum Printing and Graphics, Auburn, Maine

Printed on 80lb. Somerset Gloss, S.D. Warren Co., Skowhegan, Maine

Cover graphics, clockwise from upper left:
Circa 1950 postcard view, The Pier, Old Orchard Beach
November 1994 photo, Stonington Opera House, Stonington
April 1951 newspaper advertising art, Lewiston Drive-In Theatre, Lewiston
Circa 1950 photograph, Miss Aroostook Diner, Houlton
1961 painted label bottle, Crystal Bottling Co., Biddeford
Circa 1949 postcard view, The Sail Inn, Prospect
April 1939 advertisement, Dreamland Theatre, Livermore Falls
December 1994 photograph, Miss Portland Diner, Portland
December 1994 photograph, three waitresses, Miss Portland Diner, Portland

Table of Contents

* Still in operation

Acknowledgements

I am indebted to literally scores of people who helped me
with the research for MORE GOOD OLD MAINE. I'd like to
especially thank:

Hali Anderson-Milton, South Portland
Catherine Anderson, Rockland Public Library, Rockland
Mike Austin, Bath Assessor's Office, Bath
Kathie Barrie, Portland Public Library, Portland
Thomas C. Bennett, Portland Public Library, Portland
Mario Binette, Arundel
Gloria Bishop, Portland
Margaret Bonning, Waldoboro Public Library, Waldoboro
Terry Boober, Bangor Public Library, Bangor
Irene B. Campbell, Norway Historical Society, Norway
Marilyn Clark, Turner Memorial Library, Presque Isle
Alfred Coleman, Norwood, Ohio
Coleen Condon, Farmington Public Library, Farmington
Joan Conroy, McArthur Public Library, Biddeford
Ann Cough, Maine State Library, Augusta
Jim Cyr, Turner Memorial Library, Presque Isle
Larry Cultrera, Medford, Massachusetts
Frances DeFilipp, Mexico
Anne Dolan, *Lincoln County Weekly*, Damariscotta
Tom Gaffney, Portland Public Library, Portland
Louise Galella, Cony High School Library, Augusta
Laura Getchell-Violette, Caribou
Ellen Gingras, Lithgow Public Library, Augusta
Harold Gordon, Skowhegan
Jan Greene, Fryeburg Public Library, Fryeburg
Clayton & Nancy Gross, Deer Isle
Judy Hayes, Thompson Free Library, Dover-Foxcroft
Linda Hayman, Auburn Public Library, Auburn
Donna Hays, Bath Assessor's Office, Bath
Mike Houlihan, Town Assessor, Jay
Tom Hug, Lorain, Ohio
Diane L. Jones, Fryeburg Historical Society, Fryeburg
Erik C. Jorgensen, Pejepscot Historical Society, Brunswick
Mary Lou Kelley, Portland Public Library, Portland
Marilyn King, Caribou Public Library, Caribou
Don Larrabee, Bethesda, Maryland

Jean Libby, Rumford Public Library, Rumford
Betsy Long, Lithgow Public Library, Augusta
Susan Maxsimic, Bangor Public Library, Bangor
Barbara McIntosh, *Lewiston Sun-Journal*, Lewiston
Lorraine McQuarrie, Cary Library, Houlton
Peter Moore, York
Sharon Mrowka, McArthur Public Library, Biddeford
Dottie Murchison, Lincoln Memorial Library, Lincoln
Christine Nelson, Lincoln Memorial Library, Lincoln
Sharon Packer, Auburn
Marlene Parent, Springvale Public Library, Springvale
Elaine Parker, South Portland Public Library, South Portland
Carol Phelps, Auburn Public Library, Auburn
Rick Poore, Standish
Greg Prince, *Beverage World* magazine, Great Neck, N.Y.
Van Reid, Damariscotta
Charles Richelieu, Bath Historical Society, Bath
Joan Ricker, Turner
Dick Shaw, Bangor
Helen Shaw, Skowhegan Public Library, Skowhegan
Earle Shuttleworth, Maine Historic Preservation Commission,
Augusta
Richard Sibley, Waterville Public Library, Waterville
Nancy Skidgel, Maine State Library, Augusta
Lyn Smith, Pittsfield Public Library, Pittsfield
Virginia Spiller, Old York Historical Society, York
Gerry Spooner, Buck Memorial Library, Bucksport
Betty Tracy, Walker Memorial Library, Westbrook
Virginia Urbanek, Houlton
Ann Walsh, Portland Public Library, Portland
Claire Ward, Lewiston Public Library, Lewiston
Barbara Water, Fryeburg Public Library, Fryeburg
Arlene Welch, Caribou Public Library, Caribou
Ellen Welsh, Skidompha Public Library, Damariscotta
Glen Wheaton, Pittsfield
Frank Woodworth, Pittsfield

And **SPECIAL THANKS** to all 34 people who were wonderful enough to lend me
a photo or a postcard or a label. **MORE GOOD OLD MAINE** is far from just a
"picture book"...but it sure wouldn't be the same without the pictures, either.

Preface

When I wrote GOOD OLD MAINE in 1992-1993 I intended it to be a one-time affair. Instead it served to whet my appetite. Maine has had - and continues to have - such a wealth of pop delights that I wanted to explore more. To document - and pay tribute to - more of the grand old theatres, diners, restaurants, drive-ins, bottlers, etc. that have been so much a part of everyday life in the state.

Historians and social commentators tend to focus on wars and warriors, politics and such. Equally important, I think, are the places and products people enjoy(ed) daily. Or weekly. The "brighteners" of life, if you will. Why not have schoolchildren memorize the year the "talkie" was introduced (it was 1927) along with the year the Spanish-American War began (it was 1898) or the name and home town of Maine's oldest operating diner (the Palace/Biddeford) as well as the name and home town of its first governor (William King/Scarborough)? After all, why is the one really more important than the other?

What's especially gratifying is that there are so many wonderful - yes, even historic - places still in operation in Maine. Forty of the 101 places and products included in MORE GOOD OLD MAINE, for instance, are still up and running. And if we keep on supporting them we'll be able to keep on enjoying them. And they, in turn, will be able to keep on enjoying us.

Will Anderson

Portland, Maine
February 14, 1995

P.S. The year 1896 is generally considered to be the birth year of the movie theatre. What better way to celebrate this milestone - 100 years is, after all, a long, long time - than by taking in a show at one or more of Maine's still-in-operation old-time movie theatres? And if you go, go early and look around. Notice the architectural detail. Feel the history. Make an event of it.
You'll see a lot more than just a movie.

Unused tickets, circa 1950

Courtesy of Northeast Historic Film, Bucksport

Alamo Theatre
Bucksport

If the Alamo were a person it would be beaming. If it were a cat it would be purring. That's because, after almost four decades of being used as a supermarket, a bar, etc., the Alamo is going to again be used as a theatre. And a whole lot more! In fact, by the time you read this the Alamo will almost assuredly be thoroughly enjoying its newfound second life.

The Alamo was constructed by a man name H.O. Hussey in 1916. The question, of course, is why would anyone give the name "Alamo" to a theatre in Bucksport, Maine? It's a question for which there is no definitive answer. But David Weiss of Northeast Historic Film has a probable answer. "My best guess," he says, "is that it's because of the popularity of westerns at the time. 'The Alamo' was evocative of adventure, excitement, and the west." Makes sense. And it makes even more sense when David tells you there were also theatres named Alamo in Georgia, Illinois, and Washington, D.C.

H.O. and his wife May operated the Alamo until 1924. Then they sold it to Arthur Rosie, who ran it for 32 years, bringing Hollywood to Bucksport until 1956. The last show, on May 7th, starred Raymond "Perry Mason" Burr in *Godzilla, King of the Monsters*. Bob Rosie, Arthur's son and the theatre's manager, issued a closing statement that reflected the plight of many other movie houses across the land as well: "The Alamo Theatre felt that due to the advent of television and the national situation concerning movies that it was not feasible to run movies here any longer."

So the Alamo became an A & P. Then a health clinic. Then a bar.

Postcard view, circa 1950. The Alamo, complete with a rather nifty (and long-since-gone) neon sign, is to the left.

Courtesy of Northeast Historic Film

Then a video store. Then vacant. A boarded-up relic from the past. In 1992, however, the boards came down. Northeast Historic Film came to town. And the Alamo became their new home. Northeast Historic Film is a nonprofit organization founded in 1986 for "the purposes of cultural preservation and education." It seeks out and preserves films and videotapes of northern New England, and then makes them available to the public. For half a dozen years it operated out of tight quarters in Blue Hill; then decided to put in a bid for the Alamo. The theatre had been on the market for $300,000, but NHF lucked out and purchased it for the 1916-like price of $37,500 at a Casco Northern Bank foreclosure auction.

When I spoke with David Weiss, executive director of NHF, in late November of 1994, he was delighted at how everything was coming together. David is 40 and came to Bucksport by way of Portland, Oregon (where he was born and raised), Brown University (where he went to college, majoring in film study), Boston (where he was a filmmaker), and, of course, Blue Hill. David's wife and partner at NHF is 38-year old Karen Sheldon, a native of Montreal and Baltimore and a veteran of WGBH-TV in Boston. Karen's happy, too. They both have good reason to be. They needed space

to expand. They wanted a fire-proof building. And they wanted to be accessible to the public. The Alamo fits the bill perfectly all around. Plus, what better place for a film archives than in a former movie theatre...and a mighty good-looking one at that?

The re-born Alamo will again be a theatre, too. When I visited with David and Karen in late 1994, construction was literally going on as we spoke: a construction crew was carving a new auditorium out of what was left after the building's supermarket and barroom days. The theatre will be an intimate one, with 130 or so seats, roughly one-fifth the seating of the Alamo in its olden days. Target date for rough completion is

early 1995; for finished completion, early 1996. The "new Alamo" will feature silent movies and films made in or about Maine. But, David adds, there may well be new releases several nights a week during the summer (i.e., tourist) season. "There's plenty of room for the hall to be used for what the community wants," he sums up.

The tale of the Alamo is a wonderful one, with David and Karen's excitement matched by the excitement of the community. And whether that "community" is Bucksport and environs, all of Maine, or movie aficionados everywhere, it's great to know that the future won't just be a case of "Remember the Alamo"... it'll be a case of utilizing and enjoying it.

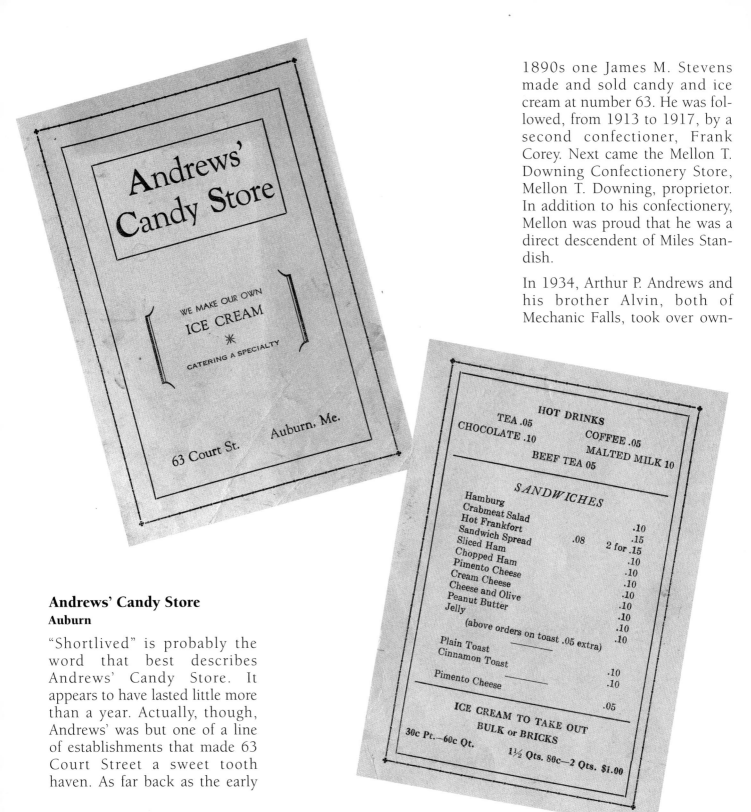

Andrews'
Candy Store

WE MAKE OUR OWN
ICE CREAM
✳
CATERING A SPECIALTY

63 Court St.   Auburn, Me.

1890s one James M. Stevens made and sold candy and ice cream at number 63. He was followed, from 1913 to 1917, by a second confectioner, Frank Corey. Next came the Mellon T. Downing Confectionery Store, Mellon T. Downing, proprietor. In addition to his confectionery, Mellon was proud that he was a direct descendent of Miles Standish.

In 1934, Arthur P. Andrews and his brother Alvin, both of Mechanic Falls, took over own-

Andrews' Candy Store
Auburn

"Shortlived" is probably the word that best describes Andrews' Candy Store. It appears to have lasted little more than a year. Actually, though, Andrews' was but one of a line of establishments that made 63 Court Street a sweet tooth haven. As far back as the early

HOT DRINKS

TEA .05
CHOCOLATE .10   COFFEE .05
                       MALTED MILK 10
BEEF TEA 05

SANDWICHES

Hamburg		.10
Crabmeat Salad		.15
Hot Frankfort		2 for .15
Sandwich Spread	.08	
Sliced Ham		.10
Chopped Ham		.10
Pimento Cheese		.10
Cream Cheese		.10
Cheese and Olive		.10
Peanut Butter		.10
Jelly		.10

(above orders on toast .05 extra)

Plain Toast
Cinnamon Toast   .10

Pimento Cheese   .10

                        .05

ICE CREAM TO TAKE OUT
BULK or BRICKS
30c Pt.—60c Qt.
1½ Qts. 80c—2 Qts. $1.00

ership, had barely enough time to print up a supply of the menu reproduced here, and then faded back to Mechanic Falls by late 1935 or so. As short as was its life, Andrews' is still recalled as an Edward Little hangout. As Connie Rogers, now 73, puts it: "It was a gathering place...where you might have a frappe or a sundae or a Pepsi." She also recalls that it had a fountain, "a lot of booths," and that it was "not decorated too much."

After Andrews', 63 Court saw service as Swan's Soda Shop, with Maynard Swan the proprietor. That would have been from late 1935 through 1939. Last call was the Grotto, also a candy and confectionery shop, operated by William Weatherbee in 1940-1941. By 1942, 63 Court Street stood vacant, and it and the rest of what was officially known as the Stevens Block was demolished later that same year. The site is now occupied by a Casco Bank building.

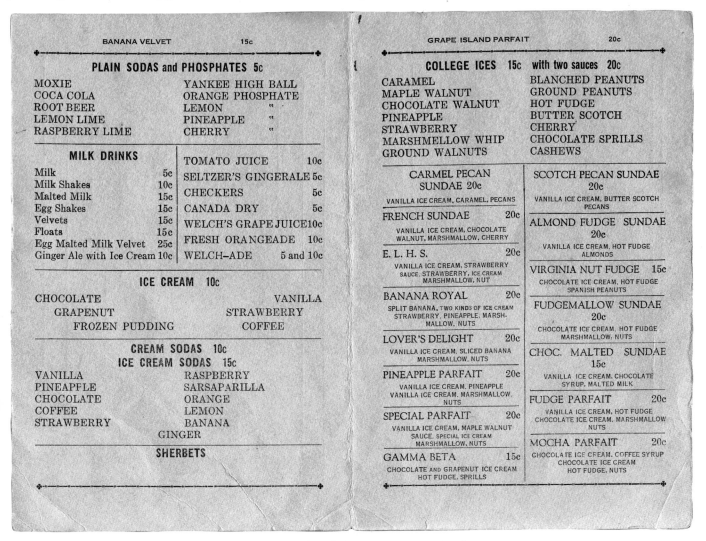

BANANA VELVET   15c   GRAPE ISLAND PARFAIT   20c

PLAIN SODAS and PHOSPHATES 5c

MOXIE	YANKEE HIGH BALL
COCA COLA	ORANGE PHOSPHATE
ROOT BEER	LEMON "
LEMON LIME	PINEAPPLE "
RASPBERRY LIME	CHERRY "

MILK DRINKS

Milk	5c	TOMATO JUICE	10c
Milk Shakes	10c	SELTZER'S GINGERALE	5c
Malted Milk	15c	CHECKERS	5c
Egg Shakes	15c	CANADA DRY	5c
Velvets	15c	WELCH'S GRAPE JUICE	10c
Floats	15c	FRESH ORANGEADE	10c
Egg Malted Milk Velvet	25c	WELCH-ADE	5 and 10c
Ginger Ale with Ice Cream	10c		

ICE CREAM 10c

CHOCOLATE	VANILLA
GRAPENUT	STRAWBERRY
FROZEN PUDDING	COFFEE

CREAM SODAS 10c
ICE CREAM SODAS 15c

VANILLA	RASPBERRY
PINEAPPLE	SARSAPARILLA
CHOCOLATE	ORANGE
COFFEE	LEMON
STRAWBERRY	BANANA
GINGER	

SHERBETS

COLLEGE ICES 15c   with two sauces 20c

CARAMEL	BLANCHED PEANUTS
MAPLE WALNUT	GROUND PEANUTS
CHOCOLATE WALNUT	HOT FUDGE
PINEAPPLE	BUTTER SCOTCH
STRAWBERRY	CHERRY
MARSHMELLOW WHIP	CHOCOLATE SPRILLS
GROUND WALNUTS	CASHEWS

CARMEL PECAN SUNDAE 20c
VANILLA ICE CREAM, CARAMEL, PECANS

FRENCH SUNDAE   20c
VANILLA ICE CREAM, CHOCOLATE WALNUT, MARSHMALLOW, CHERRY

E. L. H. S.   20c
VANILLA ICE CREAM, STRAWBERRY SAUCE, STRAWBERRY, ICE CREAM MARSHMALLOW, NUT

BANANA ROYAL   20c
SPLIT BANANA, TWO KINDS OF ICE CREAM STRAWBERRY, PINEAPPLE, MARSHMALLOW, NUTS

LOVER'S DELIGHT   20c
VANILLA ICE CREAM, SLICED BANANA MARSHMALLOW, NUTS

PINEAPPLE PARFAIT   20c
VANILLA ICE CREAM, PINEAPPLE VANILLA ICE CREAM, MARSHMALLOW, NUTS

SPECIAL PARFAIT   20c
VANILLA ICE CREAM, MAPLE WALNUT SAUCE, SPECIAL ICE CREAM MARSHMALLOW, NUTS

GAMMA BETA   15c
CHOCOLATE AND GRAPENUT ICE CREAM HOT FUDGE, SPRILLS

SCOTCH PECAN SUNDAE 20c
VANILLA ICE CREAM, BUTTER SCOTCH PECANS

ALMOND FUDGE SUNDAE 20c
VANILLA ICE CREAM, HOT FUDGE ALMONDS

VIRGINIA NUT FUDGE   15c
CHOCOLATE ICE CREAM, HOT FUDGE SPANISH PEANUTS

FUDGEMALLOW SUNDAE 20c
CHOCOLATE ICE CREAM, HOT FUDGE MARSHMALLOW, NUTS

CHOC. MALTED SUNDAE 15c
VANILLA ICE CREAM, CHOCOLATE SYRUP, MALTED MILK

FUDGE PARFAIT   20c
VANILLA ICE CREAM, HOT FUDGE CHOCOLATE ICE CREAM, MARSHMALLOW NUTS

MOCHA PARFAIT   20c
CHOCOLATE ICE CREAM, COFFEE SYRUP CHOCOLATE ICE CREAM HOT FUDGE, NUTS

Menu, 1934-1935. "College Ice" was an early term for what we now call a sundae. According to the *Dictionary of American Regional English*, it was an expression that dates back to at least 1913, and was used primarily in New England.

Augusta Drive-In Theatre
Manchester

"Everybody Everywhere Eagerly Anxiously Awaits The Gala Opening Of New England's Finest Drive-In Theatre": so rang out teaser ads in July 1950. And, on August 4th, Boston-based E.M. Loew did indeed open what they also billed as "America's Most Modern Drive-In!" Featuring the very latest RCA in-car speakers, extra-wide auto ramps, the "world's largest screen," and room for 750 cars, the Augusta Drive-In was quite a showplace. "That was *the* place to be back in those days," recalls 59-year old Augusta native Gerry Ladd. "Everybody went there, and not only for the movies: it was a big social place."

Eventually, as with so many other drive-ins, the "big social" came to an end. Rental movies and multi-screen indoor theatres proved too formidable. The Augusta Drive-In closed in September 1983. Today the theatre's former concession stand/projection booth still stands. Look for it behind the J&S/Coastal/Ultra Convenience/Ultra Kleen Car Wash complex on Route 100/202.

Aunt Martha's
Cape Neddick

What became Aunt Martha's reputedly began as a roadside lunch stand known as the Anchor Grove. In the early 1920s it was purchased by George Atherton of Cape Neddick. He enlarged the structure and changed its name to Aunt Martha's, presumably after his aunt, whose name, of course, was Martha.

Aunt Martha's was known for its "cooked electrically" meals and its picnic grounds, and its wonderful breads, rolls, pastries, and ice cream, all made daily right there at the restaurant. According to York historian John Bardwell, Aunt M's was one of the few good eating places between Boston and Portland, and did a "lively business."

George's daughter Bea ran the restaurant from 1945 to 1960. She then sold to June Collopy...but with the proviso that the name "Aunt Martha's" not be used.

Since 1960 the restaurant, on the west side of U.S. Route 1, has been known as Surfwood and has been operated on and off. When I visited in August of 1994, it was "off."

Courtesy of Maine Historic Preservation Commission, Augusta

Circa 1945 postcard view. "From a sandwich to a full course dinner" promises the words on the card's address side.

Bangor Bottling Company
Bangor

What became the Bangor Bottling Company began, circa 1899, as a small concern called Murdock & Freeman. Located at 12 Front Street, it was a branch of a company of the same name in Portland. Elvin Torrey was branch manager until 1903. Then he bought out Murdock and Freeman's Bangor plant, becoming the Bangor Bottling Company. Torrey ran the show until 1917 when the firm gained both a new address, 24 Post Office Square, and new proprietors, Thomas "Tony" McAloon and Patrick Geagan. McAloon and Geagan added such then-national brands as Hires, Whistle, and Whiz to their own Arctic Spring line. Business grew, and in 1924 Bangor Bottling moved to larger quarters at 6-8 Spring Street. An article later that same year stated the company employed seven and "requires three motor trucks to deliver Whistle, Whiz and the other goods."

Patrick Geagan died in 1941; Tony McAloon in 1947. Patrick's brothers, William and John, took over until 1952 when they sold out to Tony Rogers. Rogers, a former teacher, operated out of 6-8 Spring Street until 1958, then moved Bangor Bottling one more time, to a building he owned at 408-416 Harlow Street. It was to be the company's last move. Tony kept Bangor Bottling, by then also known as Arctic Spring Bottling, afloat until 1970. He then folded the company. Now 78, he's still alive and well in Bangor. He recalls that the biggest problem was returnable bottles that didn't get returned; that he had to go into the wholesale pizza business to keep the bottling operation going as long as he did; and that his years at the helm of Bangor Bottling "weren't great years."

"The Family Size Bottle"

CONTENTS 1 PT. 10 FL. OZ.

ARCTIC SPRING
TRADE MARK

MADE WITH ARCTIC SPRING WATER

BEVERAGES

FLAVOR DESIGNATED ON CROWN

BANGOR BOTTLING COMPANY,
McALOON & GEAGAN, PROPRIETORS
BANGOR, MAINE.

Label, circa 1940. Courtesy of Dick Shaw, Bangor

Start right and keep it up
Drink Hires Rootbeer.

Here's a lark for laughter—
Bobby up a tree.
What's the rascal after?
Surely you can see.
Just a selfish pleasure—
Thinks nobody near
To share the smallest measure
Of HIRES ROOTBEER.
Took a sip and hid it
With enjoyment sly,
Saying as he did it,
"My!
My!
My!"

Page from Hires' advertising booklet, circa 1900. Hires, first formulated by Charles E. Hires in Philadelphia in 1876, was long a top seller for the Bangor Bottling Company.

Photo, July 1994. Behind this meek and unassuming facade at 41 Sewall Street there lurks over five decades of chocolate and vanilla and coffee ripple and rum raisin and...

Barnes' Ice Cream
Augusta

What is locally celebrated, tastes great, and has been handmade in the basement of a house in Augusta for over 50 years? The answer, of course, is Barnes' Ice Cream.

Actually, Barnes' began in the basement of a store. Harland and Phoebe Barnes ran Barnes' Cash Store on Bridge Street in Augusta. The store included a soda fountain and the Barnes used Sealtest Ice Cream. Son Carl, fresh out of Cony High School, was not impressed. Said he: "I can make better ice cream." And so he did. That was 1935. Before long people from all over Augusta and beyond were waiting in line for Carl's ice cream.

In 1943, when Carl was drafted, he moved his ice cream machinery into the basement of the house he and his wife Betty shared on Sewall Street, and Betty took over as ice cream maker.

Today, 52 years later, very little has changed. Sure, Carl reverted back to being ice cream maker when he returned from the service, with Betty resuming her role as business manager. But the basement is the same, the machinery is the same, and the recipes - you bet! - are the same. The major change is that the Barnes now make a lot more flavors - 50 or so over the course of the year - but good old vanilla is still the number one best seller. The other change is distribution: for a time the Barnes flirted with statewide distribution. But in their heart of hearts they firmly believe that small is better. The result is that Barnes' Ice Cream is now basically available only in Augusta. Carl and Betty's son Richard, 48, handles distribution to local outlets and also operates an ice cream store on outer Eastern Avenue/Route 17. The Barnes sell right out of the basement, too. And that's a real treat: when you drop in it's as if you're seeing the making of

Courtesy of Betty and Carl Barnes, Augusta

In 1949-1950, Carl and Betty had a pair of trucks made for them by Refrigerated Body, Inc., of Woburn, Mass. This is truck number one as it gleamed the day the Barnes picked it up.

People around Augusta who remember the Barnes' trucks will most likely also remember the red stick: if you bought a Barnes' Ice Cream on a stick and that stick was red you received your next ice cream free. Another wonderful tradition was Barnes' apple cider popsicles. They'd make up a batch - from fresh cider, of course - every year at Halloween and give them away. Kids came from far and wide.

14

history as well as the making of ice cream.

How long will Carl and Betty, both now 82, continue to make ice cream? Who knows. But it's clearly in their blood and they clearly have a great feeling for it. As Betty says: "We just go from day to day. We were supposed to have retired years ago. We just enjoy doing it."

Belanger's Grill
Madison

You could certainly call Joe Belanger a fixture on the scene. He opened his Belanger's Grill in 1931 and, serving just plain good food and plenty of it, he remained in business three and half decades, finally closing in 1965. The building the Grill occupied was destroyed by fire several years later. Its site, 39 Main Street, is now a parking lot just to the left of Joy's Elm House Laundromat.

Circa 1940 matchbook cover

Bijou Theatre
Pittsfield

A theatre named the Bijou was opened in Pittsfield in October of 1913. This original Bijou, however, was located on Park Street on the first floor of what had been the Pittsfield House. Proprietors were Hollis Stitham and Niam Karam (later to become far better known as the local agent for both Nash and Dodge automobiles). The second Bijou, the Bijou that was to serve Pittsfield for almost six decades, came into being in a roundabout manner sometime later. A man named Andrew St. Leger opened what he named, appropriately enough, Leger's Theatre, at 69 Main Street, on August 14, 1915. Two and a half years later, in March 1918, Hollis Stitham took over the theatre as lessee…and changed its name to the Bijou (actually, the New Bijou at first to distinguish it from the original Bijou, which was closed). In January 1923, Stitham went one step further: he bought the theatre from St. Leger.

The next significant happening in the life of the Bijou came in 1929 when the theatre was converted to sound. Talkies had come to Pittsfield! "Where Talkies Sound Best" was, in fact, the Bijou's slogan for a number of years into the 1930s.

In 1956-57 the theatre was completely renovated and modern-

Cover, coming attractions flyer, 1948

ized under new proprietor J.R. Cianchette. "Full air conditioning and luxurious surroundings provide the latest and best in spectator comfort," boasted *The Pittsfield Advertiser*, further declaring the theatre to be "the most modern in Maine."

But all was not to be bliss, even for "the most modern" theatre. Two years earlier, in 1955, Andrew St. Leger (the very same man who'd built the theatre) had stepped down as manager of the Bijou after 22 years on the job. He listed competition from television, night baseball, and drive-in theatres as industry trouble spots, adding that daylight savings time had an injurious effect as well. He was correct, of course, and by the mid-1970s the Bijou was hurting. By then Millinocket native Glen Wheaton, who'd purchased the theatre in 1966, was owner and manager. As he saw it, the only way to keep the Bijou afloat was to play x-rated movies. And that he flat out refused to do.

Because of his stand, Glen Wheaton became somewhat of a celebrity around central Maine. But fame doesn't necessarily get the bills paid. As the *Maine Sunday Telegram* put it in December of 1971: "While townspeople loudly applaud Wheaton's position, they are not exactly standing in line to get into the Bijou." The result was a moral - but not a financial - victory. Glen closed the Bijou in late March 1975.

All was not to be lost, however. Heeding Wheaton's plea, the Pittsfield branch of Maine Savings Bank and the Cianbro Corporation joined forces to purchase the theatre, and donate it to the Town of Pittsfield. The outcome was - and is - the Pittsfield Community Theatre, a non-profit community endeavor with movies, legitimate theatre, stage shows, even the annual Central Maine Egg Festival's Princess Pageant. Has the Community Theatre been all wine and roses? Nope. "We're swimming upstream against the videos," admitted Pittsfield Community Theatre Vice-Chairman Don Hallenbeck when I spoke with him in October of 1994. "But," he was quick to add, "we're still operating in the black. We're holding our own."

Blethen House
Dover-Foxcroft

What do you do if you're young and impetuous and you see a 150-year-old hotel and you fall in love with it? Well, if you're Karl Cousins, you buy it. As Karl, 26, tells it: "I happened to be driving through Dover-Foxcroft and I happened to see the Blethen House, and I said, 'Wow, what a beautiful building." At first all Karl wanted to do was view the hotel; to take a tour of it. He makes it very clear that he had no intention of buying it. None whatsoever. But then he fell in love with it. The clincher came when he heard that the town was thinking of tearing the hotel down. "I was like the fish who just wants to see the worm... and then gets hooked," he analogizes.

Actually, Karl didn't get hooked alone. The buying of the Blethen House, in August of 1993, was very definitely a family affair, and brothers Lee, 27, and Eddie, 24, and sister Anna-Lisa, 21, are very definitely a part of the commitment to making the continuing story of the Blethen House a story with a happy ending.

The Blethen House has roots that go back to 1842. That was the year Major Issac Blethen constructed what he named the Tremont House. This structure, located across East Main Street, was moved in 1843 and now forms part of the present-day

Photo, October 1994. The Pittsfield Community Theatre, nee the Bijou, is nestled between the T.F. Connor Building, built in 1913, on the left, and the Perkins Building, built in 1851, on the right. It's a nice fit.

BLETHEN HOUSE - DOVER, ME.

Postcard view, circa 1900. I like this card for both its message and the fact that it nicely combines Dover and Foxcroft, sort of a pre-saging of the year, 1922, when the two would join together to become Dover-Foxcroft. The message is on the "front" of the card because that was then the law of the land: prior to 1907, postal requirements prohibited all but the sendee's name and address on the "back" side.

Blethen House. In 1860 the building was enlarged to three stories. It also gained the name - the Blethen House - that it's had ever since. In 1880, the building was enlarged again, to four stories.

At first, according to William R. Sawtell in his book *The Blethen House: Tale of a Survivor*, the hotel catered to the stagecoach trade. It was an important stop on the Bangor to Moosehead Lake run, and was also the starting point for the stage to Dexter.

Issac Blethen ran the Blethen house for its first decade. His son William then took over management and ran the hotel until he died in 1907. An article written in 1899 lauded the Blethen house thusly: "It is fighting blood that wins battles and it is the hotel blood in the Blethen family that enables them to manage their hotel as they do." Con-tinued the article: "The whole house is modern in every partic-ular. All guests enjoy the fine cuisine and service, and have an advantage of inestimable impor-tance of pure air, pure spring water, and perfect sanitary con-ditions, and a fine livery for the charming drives in the vicinity, making it an ideal place for the tourist and commercial traveler." A 1907 ad further glorified the Blethen House, claiming it to be "The Best Appointed and Most Complete Hotel in Eastern Maine."

In April of 1931 a fire badly damaged the Blethen House. Management, however, wasted no time in putting the hotel back in order. When it reopened in August, *The Piscataquis Obser-vor* reported that "A housewarm-ing was given the proprietors by the people of Dover-Foxcroft." The article added that "It must be said that the hotel never looked lovelier."

In 1936 ownership of the Blethen House passed out of the control of the Blethen family. Percy Stacy, a native of Blan-chard, Maine, and a veteran of the hotel business, became the new proprietor. But the Blethen tradition was maintained. Guests were treated as family, not as customers. The hotel's cuisine was unsurpassed and, again according to William R. Sawtell, "People came to the hotel from everywhere to eat in the dining room."

In 1954 the Blethen House changed hands again. The new proprietor was Paul Plourde.

Ad, 1961. The Blethen House was long noted for its natural spring water piped into each and every room.

Plourde brought with him a seemingly strange background. Born in Van Buren in 1913, he grew up on a farm. At age 19 he left Van Buren for the brighter lights of Rockland, where he practiced barbering for 20-odd years. In fact, when Paul Plourde took over the hotel and people asked "Who is he?," the response was often "He's a good barber."

As it turned out, though, Paul Plourde made the perfect host. Seventy-nine year old Carl Lutterell, who worked at the Blethen House for 30 years, recalls the Plourde years well. The dining room was packed. "If you didn't have a reservation on a Thursday, Friday, or Saturday, you didn't get in." Sunday, with

Photos, November 1994, with Karl, left, and Eddie on the balcony of their "baby." When I spoke with Karl in November of 1994 he reported that "Business is ok, but I wouldn't go so far as to say it's booming." The younger folks in town - the 20-40 age group - are skeptical. "They basically think we're nuts," laughs Karl. "But the older generation are totally behind us. They come in and patronize us and say how good it looks."

chicken and lobster dinners the specialty of the kitchen, was extremely popular, too. "These older women from Bangor, Lincoln, Skowhegan, and Waterville would drive over in their big cars on Sunday. Sometimes," and here Carl gives a big grin, "he (Paul) would give 'em a little pat on the rear, and he'd use his French accent, and they'd love it."

Paul Plourde retired, at age 67, in 1980. In the years since, before the arrival of the Cousins, the stately old hotel saw several proprietors. None were overly successful, and, sad but true, the Blethen house stood vacant for the better part of a year before Karl's fortuitous drive through Dover-Foxcroft.

It's enjoyed quite a past, but what's much more exciting about the Blethen House is its present. And, of far greater importance, its future. Karl and Lee and Eddie, all natives of East Millinocket and all UMO graduates, are fully commited to the hotel and to its restoration. Karl and Lee live on premises and put in a 15-18 hour day. Every day. They know it'll be like that for a solid five to ten years. But that's ok. Karl, especially, loves history and the fact that he's doing his best to preserve a piece of it. "We have a big task on our hands," he admits, "but there's a lot of beauty. You have to be able to project ahead... to what it's going to look like."

Postcard view, circa 1930. The Bowlodrome was a bowling alley and a whole lot more. Once described as "the outstanding example of brickwork in Maine," it is a delight to behold. *Courtesy of Maine Historic Preservation Commission, Augusta*

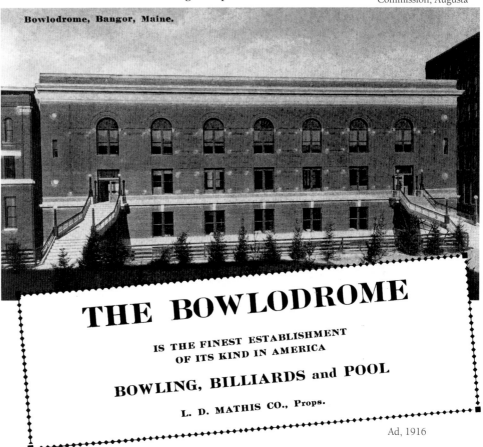

Bowlodrome, Bangor, Maine.

THE BOWLODROME

IS THE FINEST ESTABLISHMENT OF ITS KIND IN AMERICA

BOWLING, BILLIARDS and POOL

L. D. MATHIS CO., Props.

Ad, 1916

The Bowlodrome
Bangor

When I first laid eyes upon the postcard above, I said "No way. There is no way a building that looks like a cross between Fenway Park and the world's biggest Y.M.C.A. could be a bowling alley."

Well, I was right and I was wrong. Part of the building was a bowling alley; other parts were used for other purposes. The Bowlodrome part opened for business in May of 1915. Advertised as "Bangor's Palatial New Amusement Center," it featured nine bowling alleys and ten billiard/pool tables. Three of the nine alleys were "reserved for ladies." Bowling cost 10¢ a string; billiards/pool, 60¢ an hour. Lorenzo D. Mathis, of Portland, was proprietor.

But the Bowlodrome was not alone in the Bowlodrome building. The level below the alleys was originally utilized by the Knowles & Dow Buick showroom. Above were floors that became home to boxing and wrestling, and to dancing. It's the dancing that people remember most.

The Chateau - that was the ballroom's name - was on the top floor. It was apropos, because that made it just a little closer to heaven. Just the way the older people I spoke with recall it. "It was delightful, with a big revolving light on the ceiling," reminisces 79-year-old Winn native Phillip Jarvis, who used to go to the Chateau in the early 1930s. Hilda Wardwell, 71, of Bangor, recalls the ceiling light as well. "There was a big ball in the center of the dance hall which spun around and gave off glistening lights." Hilda confesses, though, that the Chateau had more going for it than just its revolving light: " It was a bit of a risqué place. My mother didn't approve of my going unless I was with a group, never alone or with just another female friend. It was considered rather a fast place in those days (1939-1945)." Sixty-four year old Ruth Bracy of Bangor also recalls the Chateau as a good place to be: "I couldn't dance very well and I was a horrible bowler, but I went there to watch. There used to be some marvelous dancers there. It was fun to just sit and watch them. And that's how I learned (to dance). I figured if they can do

it so can I." My favorite recollection, however, comes from 70-year old Bangor native Bob Taylor. Bob bowled at the Bowlodrome, danced and even roller-skated at the Chateau. His eyes light up when he thinks back to the beauty of the dance floor, with its high ceilings and ornate plaster designs. And its acoustics. "The acoustics were wonderful," he reminisces. "And on a hot summer night they'd open the windows... and you could hear music all over downtown Bangor."

The music stopped in 1948. The bowling, too. Sears took a lease on the Bowlodrome building, turning it into an annex of their store on Harlow Street. Easy-chairs and washing machines replaced bowlers and dancers. Eventually Sears moved out - moved to the mall - and the Bowlodrome Building then sat vacant and slowly rotting.

In 1992, however, there was born a vision called Norumbega Hall, a rebirth of the Bowlodrome building (also known as the Morse Building) and its neighbor, the Central Block Building. The creation of 41-year old Bowdoin grad and writer/entrepreneur Robert Duerr, it will feature offices and shops and convention facilities. It will be beautiful.

Will music be heard again all over downtown Bangor? You never know.

Artist's sketch, Norumbega Hall Project, 1994. The former Bowlodrome building is to the right.

Courtesy of Robert Duerr, Bangor.

Bridgton Drive-In Theatre

Bridgton

John Tevanian could easily be called Mr. Maine Drive-In Movie Theatre Man. He's been involved with the ownership and operation of four "ozoners" through the years. There's been the Kennebunk Drive-In, the Windham Drive-In, the Pride's Corner Drive-In, and the Bridgton Drive-In. All but the last were Tevanian *family* enterprises, run with John's brothers, Herb and Al, and their respective wives and children. That was fine as far as it went, but there came a time when John felt hemmed in. As he explains it: "It was getting too crowded with family members. I wanted to get out and do my own thing." That's just what John did, purchasing the Bridgton Drive-In - which dates back to 1957-1958 when it was constructed by Russell Martin of Sanford - in 1971. The Portland native, with considerable help from his sons, John S., 26, and Andy, 25, has been operating the drive-in ever since. And loving it. "I'm having about as much fun as the people who come in

Marquee, June 1994. When I interviewed John and John S. in mid-June, 1994, they were thrilled to be about to run *Wolf*, starring Jack Nicholson and Michelle Pfeiffer, on the film's national release date... the exact same day as the big, high-powered theatres all across the land. The Bridgton Drive-In was, in effect, a part of a World Premiere.

Sign at entrance to theatre, June 1994. John states flat out: "We're the best entertainment value in the State of Maine."

here," he radiates, continuing: "It's a fun business. You never really know what's going to happen."

John does a lot of family business, families who are, he says, "thankful that there is still this type of entertainment." And John delights at the goodly number of patrons - especially, he notes, summer people from Massachusetts - who come and bring their kids and say "This is what *we* did when *we* were kids."

21

Photo, circa 1923, showing Burnell's Place as it appeared in the beginning. Left to right is an unidentified employee, Arthur, Sr., and Harriet.

All photos courtesy of Pearl and Arthur Burnell, Jr., South Portland.

Sr. pumped a lot of gas and sold a lot of food. "Mostly he served hot dogs and hamburgers and fried clams," Arthur, Jr. recalls. "My mother, Harriet, did the cooking."

Circa 1927 Arthur, Sr. and Harriet added a half-dozen or so cabins to their venture. Plus they enlarged their restaurant. A 1929 ad touts Burnell's cabins as the "Most Up-To-Date in New England," with hot and cold water and shower baths and "Beds That Assure Real Restful Sleep." Lunches and fried clams were served "At All Hours."

Business boomed during the 1930s. It may have been the Depression, but the tourists still

Burnell's Place
Scarborough

"He had that land and there were no gas stations around." So explains Arthur Burnell, Jr., 83, as to why his father, Arthur Burnell, Sr., opened a place in 1922 that is still more or less in operation today.

"That land" was three acres fronting on Saco Road, better known as U.S. Route 1, in Scarborough. Arthur, Sr. purchased the property circa 1920 and by 1922 he figured it was time to make something of it. So he built a two-pump filling station and a four-stool restaurant and he was in business. It was a success from the beginning. Arthur,

Photo, circa 1932, picturing a young Arthur Burnell, Jr. Arthur, Jr. didn't mind manning the pumps. Or washing dishes. Or cleaning the cabins. What he did mind was waiting on tables. Trying to keep patrons happy was not his forte. "They'd order something and they'd alter it later," he still states with conviction all these decades later.

came. And they still bought. Especially Harriet's fried clams. "They'd come back year after year for those," remembers Pearl Burnell, 75, Arthur, Jr.'s wife and a longtime Burnell's employee herself. "It was Harriet's batter that made them so good."

Burnell's, though, was more than

dining room and she'd read the paper and she was very friendly."

A highlight of a different sort came during the war years. Because of the fear of an air raid, nighttime exterior lights were forbidden. The restaurant was open, but with muted interior lights only. Arthur, Sr. was as

Photo, 1928. The newly launched cabins are to the right.

just fried clams. Pearl is quick to point out the popularity of the restaurant's steaks and full course seafood dinners. Breakfasts, too. A highlight came in the late 1930s when Eleanor Roosevelt, staying nearby at the Danish Village, ate at Burnell's Place for a whole week. Pearl recalls the first lady as "fond of the seafood" but not fond of fuss: "She didn't want any fanfare at all. She just wanted to be another customer. She ate in the

patriotic as the next man, but one dark night he let his frustrations get the better of him. "How's anybody gonna know if we're open if we don't put on the outside lights," he reasoned. So he turned them on. All of them. "You could see us clear into Portland," Pearl laughs now. But she wasn't laughing then: "I expected to hear the sirens and have Civil Defense shut us down for good."

Burnell's, though, escaped both

an air raid and the Civil Defense. What it didn't escape was next-generation apathy. When Arthur, Sr., then 68, was ready to retire in 1946, none of the family wanted to take over. The result was that Arthur, Sr. sold to a couple, Harold and Virginia Simpson, outside of the family. They changed the name to Simpson's and operated into the 1970s. James Williams then took over - changing the name again, to Jimmy's Hamburgers - and operated into the late 1980s. Since then it's been Kimball's Kitchen, TCBY of Scarborough, and, beginning in the autumn of 1994, Northern Lites Cafe. Of course, the restaurant you see now doesn't look at all like the photos shown here. The old stand has been cut up and torn down and remodeled and added to more than just a couple of times. But you have to suspect that the core, at least, of Arthur and Harriet's dream is still there somewhere.

Photo, circa 1935, with Harriet on the left and her sister-in-law Adelaide second from the right.

Photo, circa 1932, with Arthur, Sr. seated on the right. In the rear can be seen the dining room. That was Arthur's real love. Pearl recalls that "It had nice table-cloths and everything had to be spic 'n span. If he (Arthur, Sr.) saw a spot (on the tablecloth) he'd yank that tablecloth out and let you know it."

Capitol Diner
Augusta

"Modern, with stainless steel and chrome. Real fancy.": that's how 74-year old Gabe Betit remembers the Capitol. He should know. From 1934 to 1938, after his day as a student at Cony High, he set pins at nearby Market Square Alleys. He'd wind down at midnight. Then, finances allowing, it was over to the diner for a healthy helping of pie. Custard was his favorite.

The Capitol Diner was started by a man named William Tuttle in 1934. In 1936, Tuttle sold to a William Bell, who ran the diner for the better part of a decade, until 1945. Bert and Rita Ouellette then became the proprietors. But for Bert, fresh out of the Navy, the diner was just someplace he viewed as a stepping stone to bigger and better things. "He wanted to own a regular restaurant," 73-year old Rita recalls. The result was that the couple sold the Capitol to Rita's brother, Clem Doyan. That was in 1947.

Under Clem the Capitol continued to be noted for its pies. Apple and blueberry. Sure. And Gabe Betit's old favorite, custard, too. But the real favorites were the meat pies—tourtieres—as well as chicken and salmon pies.

Clem Doyon suffered a stroke in 1968 at age 52, causing him to close the diner. It sat vacant on its Cony Hill site for several

Photo, circa 1946: Clem's sister, Gert Davis, poses outside the Capitol with her infant son, Wayne. The Capitol was a Sterling, manufactured by the Sterling Dining Car Company (a.k.a. J.B. Judkins Co.) of Merrimac, Massachusetts.

Courtesy of
Rita Ouellette, Augusta

years. Then the City of Augusta purchased and demolished it as part of the plans for the eventual construction of a new City Hall. The Capitol's former site, at 30 Cony Avenue, is today occupied by a grassy area just to the left of the entranceway for that new City Hall.

Ad, 1952. You have to like Clem Doyon's slogan! But while Clem is real proud of his cooking, it's actually the friends that he made that he most recalls from his 22 years in the diner trade. Interviewed in July 1994, he simply said: "Meeting nice people; making a lot of friends." That's what meant the most to him.

Cascade Lodge and Cabins
Saco

A "landmark": that's the word that Richard S. Aube, co-owner since 1985, uses to characterize the Cascade. He's right. The Cascade is one of those places that's seemingly been around forever. It would be difficult to imagine Route 1 without it.

There would most likely be no Cascade, however, if it were not for a man named Burland H. Hawkes. Born in Westbrook in

Matchbook cover, circa 1938. On the inside cover is advertised "Daily Special Dinners at 75¢ to $2.50."

1898, Hawkes graduated from Westbrook High, then worked for the A.H. Berry Shoe Company of Portland until April of 1930, when he traded the shoe business for the tourist business. He took the position of manager at the brand-new Cascade Lodge and Cabins. Before long, B.H. (he seldom used his full first name) was president and treasurer as well.

Early advertisements describe the Cascade's main lodge as "combining country club with hotel" with respect to accommodations, while chicken, steak, and shore dinners - topped off with all-homemade pastry - were the specialties of the kitchen. Thirty-four single and double cabins fanned out beside and behind the lodge, with each "a separate, self-contained and privately situated domicile, offering accommodations that are unexcelled anywhere." Set all of this in "rolling open country" and you have, as one write-up of the day phrased it, a location "a bit removed from the urgency of the workaday world."

A lot of workdays have come and gone along Route 1 since 1930. B.H. Hawkes sold the Cascade in 1966, and passed away in 1982. His "baby" is now owned and operated by Marie and Richard L. Aube and their son, Richard S. Aube, and it's

B.H. Hawkes believed in the power of advertising. This how-to-get-there map was included in a handsome little folder

he put out in 1935 or so. Also included was the B.H. promise "The management aims to offer something superior in wayside accommodations."

called the Cascade Inn and Restaurant. But the cabins are still there. In fact, there are 38 of them now. And the rolling open country is still there. So are the chicken, steak, and shore dinners. And the main lodge looks mighty grand...especially for a 65-year old. B.H. would be proud.

CASCADE LODGE and CABINS, Saco, Maine.

Postcard view of the main lodge, circa 1940, plus a present-day shot, June 1994. Not much has changed except the cars. And, reports Carol Aube, Cascade's Function Coordinator, there are lots and lots of people who return for that very reason. They appreciate that the Cascade remains much the same as it's always been. They recall weddings or graduations or class reunions of yesteryear. Most of all they recall standing under the portico and having their photograph taken.

Chic Theatre, Milo, Me.

Courtesy of Maine Historic Preservation Commission, Augusta

Chic Theatre
Milo

The Chic (pronounced "Chick") Theatre opened in 1913. A man with the wonderfully alliterative name of Paul P. Peaks was the first manager. After two decades, in 1932, new owners decided on a new name. The Chic Theatre became the Milo Theatre. And the Milo it would remain for the rest of its run on Main Street.

Two men who recall the theatre well are longtime employee Carl Lutterell, 79, and Milo Town Historian Ralph Monroe, 67. "It was the gathering place in town," states Ralph unequivocally. That's partially because it doubled as a bowling alley: there were two lanes, usually kept mighty busy, under the theatre. But it was mostly the movies themselves. "We'd draw from Brownville, Brownville Junction, Lagrange, Medford, and even Dover-Foxcroft (which had its own theatre)," Carl says proudly. "Roy Rogers or Gene Autry: they were always a good attraction," he continues, "and Fred Astaire and Ginger Rogers. And *Gone with the Wind*. That was a good repeat show. I can't tell you how many times I saw *Gone with the Wind*." There'd sometimes be in-person acts, too. Carl, who worked at the theatre from 1936 to 1951, especially recalls Curley O'Brien and his band from Bangor. "We really packed the place," he beams.

What Carl recalls most of all, though, is the kids. "I enjoyed the children coming to the matinee," he reminisces. "It was great to hear them holler. And to see them walk up to the ticket booth. They were really proud to have that much money to spend."

Ralph has good memories, too: how as a youngster, he'd sometimes let his buddies in gratis by opening a back door (when the manager wasn't looking, of course); how there was a drug store next to the theatre, with a doorway between the two so theatre patrons could buy candy from the candy counter (which was located - conveniently! - right by the doorway); and how the popcorn was good... "although a lot of it did get thrown off the balcony."

Ralph's favorite memory gets him laughing pretty hard. It seems on older acquaintance was making use of the theatre's rest room - which was located adjacent to the ticket booth - when he heard the show starting. Not wanting to miss anything, he rushed out before he had a chance to fully zip his

Photo, November 1994. The former theatre's still majestic false front gable - "crown," if you will - as it reaches for the sky.

fly...and ran smack into a woman "with a rather full dress" who had just purchased her ticket. His zipper got caught in her dress. The result, which Ralph still vividly recalls although we're talking 45 years or so, was that the acquaintance literally stuck with the woman and the two of them walked lockstepped down the aisle, until she went to sit down and he told her of his predicament.

The theatre closed in 1962. A major reason was the coming of the Milo Drive-In. "It was easier to load everybody into the car and go to the drive-in," Ralph recollects. There was also the fact that the theatre was getting old and rundown. Between the two, "People just stopped going," sums up Ralph.

For 32 years the Chic/Milo stood vacant. In 1994 it was purchased by Larry Boutot, of Orono. When I visited Milo in November 1994, Larry was hard at work converting the former theatre into an auction hall. While some people in town might object to the theatre's once handsome stucco facade being covered over with vinyl siding, Carl Lutterell isn't one of them. "I'm glad to see something being down with it. Anything.," he says. "It'll spruce up the main street a little."

The Chick-A-Dee
Turner

One of south central Maine's longest running roadside haunts owes its start to the strange combination of a gas war and a mother's desire to be outdoors with her child. Newlyweds Francis and Irma Donovan had purchased a filling station on Route 4 in Turner in early 1936. They sold a fair amount of gas but didn't make any money. As Irma, now 87, recounts: "We fell into a gas war and we were almost giving the gas away at 11 gallons for $1.00". Included, however, in their filling station purchase was an unfinished house. Frustrated with gas war woes, Francis and Irma converted the house into a dance hall. That, too, turned out to be not much of a profit center. "We charged 25¢ apiece admission," Irma laughs. "It was really more of a neighborhood thing; neighbors and their families." Irma didn't want to be cooped up anyway. She had just become a mother and wanted to share the great outdoors with her daughter Frances. The solution? That's simple, thought Irma. "Let's try

Courtesy of Joan Ricker, Turner

Photo, circa 1939. If you guess this is the original Chick-A-Dee you'd be close...but off by one expansion. The original was but six feet square, a miniscule structure that Francis and Irma inherited as part of their filling station venture. When the filling station proved less than fully successful, they moved what had been a shed into a prominent position by the state road, cut out one side to make way for a service window, and commenced to sell ice cream and soda pop. Business boomed, and the couple sawed their original structure in half, and then stretched it out with an entirely new section inbetween. This is the "stretched-out" version.

an ice cream and soda pop stand." And they did. "We sold ice cream cones with a cherry on top." The price was 5¢. Kids from miles around loved it. And they brought their families with them. Soon people were asking for hot dogs, too. Francis said ok...but he didn't want to do just plain old hot dogs. He said "Let's do something different: let's do 10" hot dogs and sell them for a dime." And they did. It was success story number two. People came from all over to feast. It was, after all, Depression times and it was the largest hot dog in Androscoggin County and all around and it was only 10¢. Irma smiles a good smile as she recalls two brothers from Buckfield who would arrive quite often and who really did the hot dogs justice: "Both of them could eat six or eight at one sit-

Chick-a-Dee clam claim check (try saying that quickly ten times in a row!), circa 1950.

Courtesy of Irma Donovan, Lewiston

ting. They were both big guys...but for 80¢ they could really fill up."

Other successes followed. The Donovans introduced what they called a Wimpy - a 10¢ hamburger with lettuce and tomatoes - to the area. Then came fried clams, which became the Chick-A-Dee's all-time success story. "We hired this elderly woman to cook and she could really cook clams." Irma smiles as she recollects each success along the way. But her biggest smile is reserved for romance. "We had all these young couples (as patrons) and sometimes they'd sit and enjoy the grove." And these couples would come back again and again, keeping Francis and Irma posted: "Hey, we're engaged; hey, we're married." Today, fifty and more years later, Irma still gets Christmas cards from many of these same couples. "You wouldn't believe how many," she says proudly.

Starting from a structure six feet square - Francis and Irma called it the Little Chick-A-Dee for a time - the Chick-A-Dee mushroomed. "It was just a topsy thing that grew and grew," is how Irma phrases it. Almost before they knew it cars were lined up far beyond any expectations either of them might've ever had. A lot of their growth was because of the food. But a lot of it was the setting, too. As Irma again phrases it: "We were

in the country and we had a beautiful grove (of pine trees) and people would just come and eat hot dogs and ice cream and fried clams outside." Sounds pretty good.

Today, almost 60 years later, the Chick-A-Dee is still going strong. Francis and Irma sold their creation to William Hird of Auburn in the summer or 1971. Irma has a story about that, too. "We had a realtor friend - and good customer, too - named Norm Roy. He was in the restaurant one evening and overheard someone ask Francis if he'd ever sell the Chick-A-Dee. Francis' answer was 'Yes, if they've got the money.'" Well, the very next day Norm Roy appeared again. He had a purchaser and he had the money. "We'd been in it (the business) 35 years," Irma concludes. It was time to quit.

The Chick-A-Dee of today bears no resemblance to the Chick-A-Dee of yesterday. Growth and a pair of complete-destruction fires (in 1966 and 1991) saw to that. The legacy of "Just Good Food" - especially fried clams - continues on, however. Bill Hird, with his brother Greg, represents the second generation of Hirds holding forth at what is definitely a landmark location. Here's what Bill, in 25 words or less, has to say: "The reason we stay successful is because of our consistency and the quality and quantity of our food."

Photo, 1938. The family showed up and Irma was there to take their picture. Left to right that's Irma's mother, Flora LeClair; Flora's brother, Henry Bosse; Irma's sister, Julia LeClair; Flora's brother, Wilfred Bosse; Irma's sister, Beatrice LeClair; Francis Donovan; Irma and Francis' daughter, Frances; and Irma's brother, Bernard LeClair. Francis was a native of Lewiston, Jordan High School class of 1926, and then went to UMO. Irma was a native of Lisbon but she, too, went to Jordan, class of 1928. Francis passed away in July of 1993. Irma is very much alive and well and living in Lewiston.

Courtesy of Irma Donovan, Lewiston

Irma still recalls - as if it were yesterday - how the name "Chick-A-Dee" came about. When they first had the idea of a place of their own, she recounts, she'd fire different possible names at Francis. "One day, when it was winter and slushy and he was crossing the street ahead of me, I hollered 'Chickadee'...and he hollered back, 'That's it." Irma is less sure how their place ended up being spelled the way it is, with the hyphens. She thinks "It was just one of those things: when the man painted the sign or something it ended up that way. And we left it that way." Whatever, it was obviously a good choice.

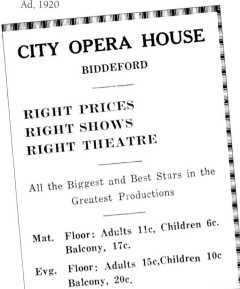

City Theater
Biddeford

It's going to take a big cake to hold all the candles. That's because in January of 1996 the City Theater will be 100 years old. Ten decades. One century. It's quite a feat.

The City Theater was born the City Opera House. And actually the theatre we know now is City Opera House II. Number one, built into City Hall, was destroyed by fire in December 1894. Biddeford spared little expense when it rebuilt. Noted Portland architect John Calvin Stevens was hired to design the new City Hall and Opera House. Stevens did not disappoint. The result was - and is - a Victorian delight. When the theatre opened on January 20th the *Biddeford Daily Journal* wrote that "Biddeford has the handsomest play-house in Maine - perhaps also the finest

this side of Boston." The paper was not far off.

Although built for vaudeville and legitimate theatre, the Opera House early-on turned to movies as well. A February 1905 ad ballyhoos "High Class Moving Pictures," further promising "Positively every Picture new and original." And well before World War I, James P. Rundle, the theatre's lessee and manager, appears to have turned predominantly to the big screen. Ads from 1912 talk up two and three reelers, "a classy selection of moving pictures," and that admission was but a nickel. The emphasis on movies notwithstanding, the Opera House (renamed City Theater in January 1926) has been host to quite a noteworthy array of live and in-person acts. Articles written

on the theatre list Charlie Chaplin, Al Jolson, W.C. Fields, Laurel and Hardy, Abbott and Costello, Fred Astaire, even Roy Rogers and his trusty horse, Trigger.

All went seemingly well until the 1960s. The City Theater then experienced the same problems felt by moviehouses nationwide. People stayed home and watched television. TV was in. Movie theatres were not. In March of 1971 the theatre's doors were closed and locked, and the theatre's marquee was labeled an eyesore by the city and torn down.

The years 1971 through 1974 can only be termed dismal. The theatre became primarily a storage depot for the city. Steve Dandy, president of the board of directors of the present-day City

Courtesy of Rick Poore, Standish

Photo, 1926, when the City Theater and Ernest L. Harmon Dodge joined forces to promote football star Harold "Red" Grange's movie debut in *One Minute To Play*. "The Galloping Ghost" would make two other films before retiring from movieland.

Theater Associates, Inc., recalls that "the stage was filled with parking meters." Worse, a local horseshoe club talked the city into letting them use the theatre for wintertime practice. They trucked in dirt and set up shop in the area in front of the stage. Just when all seemed lost, however, a group of people who gave a damn got together and decided it was time to do something. Out of this evolved City Theater Associates, a non-profit organization dedicated to the preservation and successful operation of the theatre.

In the years since, City Theater patrons have delighted to countless plays, concerts, ballets, poetry readings, and even an occasional silent movie classic or two. But the going has not always been easy. There has been conflict. And financial hardships. When I talked with Steve in October of 1994 he told me that things had been pretty bleak in the autumn of 1993. "We were close to being closed," he admitted. But, with help from Peoples Heritage Bank, the group forced themselves to cut costs, put themselves on a no-nonsense budget, and developed a five-year plan. It's paid off. Says Steve: "We now have money in the bank and that allows us to operate, and," he adds, "gives everyone involved a feeling of satisfaction."

Happy, happy 100th birthday, City Theater!

Photo, April 1994. The entrance is humble. Inside, though, there's a 684-seat National Historic Landmark theatre with accoustics so exceptional that one theatre expert declared "You could do a stage production here without any amplification, " and with turn-of-the-century detail that can only be described as truly majestic. As Steve Dandy, president of the board of directors of City Theater Associates, phrased it: "Once people get inside, they say 'Wow, where did this come from?'"

Photo, April 1994. It still says "Opera House" on the tile floor entranceway.

CLARKE'S **NORMANDIE** — WEST SCARBORO, MAINE

ROUTE I AT DUNSTON CORNER, BETWEEN BIDDEFORD AND PORTLAND

Clarke's Normandie
West Scarborough

A good 70 years ago, right around 1924, Earl Bennett and Cliff Leary got together to found what they cleverly called the Earlcliff. Specializing in fried clams, hot dogs, and homemade ice cream, the Earlcliff was one of the very first roadside restaurants in the area. Starting as take-out only, it was so successful that a full-fledged dining room was soon added. Overnight accommodations were also made available.

By 1929 Earl had bought out his partner and changed the restaurant's name to the Benway. In the 1930s it became Dunsboro Farm, with a Mrs. Zoe Morse as proprietress.

Circa 1938 Ernest and Mildred Clarke became proprietors. They changed the name to Clarke's Normandie. A 1939 ad touts luncheons at 50¢ to 90¢, and chicken, steak, and shore dinners for 75¢ all the way up to $2.00. The Clarkes operated the Normandie through most of World War II, then sold it to Louise and Joe Doyle. The Doyles maintained the Normandie name and kept things going - with chicken, steak, and shore dinners still the specialties of the house - until 1951. They then moved to Massachusetts, selling the restaurant to partners Albert York and Arthur MacPhee, who ran the by-then venerable eatery for several years as the Holiday Inn (no relation to the Holiday Inn chain, which wasn't even started until 1952). Since then the former restaurant has been home to Hartford's Used Furniture, and Oliver's TV Outlet. It is today occupied by Oliver Vending & Music Systems.

Clark's Beverages
Newcastle

Circa 1926 a young Newcastle farmer named Chester Clark bought a tiny bottling operation from Spencer Gay of Damariscotta. He set up shop in a shed behind the family homestead on River Road in Newcastle. "It was primitive," recalls Chester's daughter, Phyllis. "They used to sit me out there in a highchair while my mother, Gladys, would scrub out the bottles by hand. It was all by hand."

Painted label bottle, 1969

Phyllis has fond memories of it all, though. She smiles when asked what her favorite flavor was. "Grape. It was always grape," she replies unhesitatingly. But it was white birch beer for which Clark's was most noted: "I remember people from away would stop in on their way home and buy a case. It was unique."

Business grew and Chester and Gladys built an all new/all modern plant, still on River Road, circa 1946. In 1949, the man who would become Phyllis' husband, Win Billings, came on board. By then Clark's had a second shift. In the summer only. Win estimates that 80% of their business was summer trade, with half a dozen trucks making the rounds from Bailey Island to Belgrade Lakes to Belfast.

Chester Clark died in 1961. Gladys kept things going until 1963-1964, then sold to Bertie Scott, owner of Mack Bottling Company in Waldoboro. Bertie consolidated operations in Newcastle, remaining in business until 1976. The former River Road plant, an impressive three-story structure set on a bluff above the Damariscotta River, was home to Hanson Energy Products until recently. It is now vacant.

One event stands out in Win Billings' 27-year career with Clark's/Mack. That was DOUBLE COLA CONTEST DAY. It was Sunday, May 19, 1957. And "It was a *big* day." Clark's had unveiled a new franchised brand, Double Cola. Chester decided a contest was in order, with prizes awarded to those retail accounts that sold the most Double Cola during its introductory period. "There must have been a dozen or more prizes in all," Win recollects, with the grand prize being a clock radio. Over 100 people turned out. There were guided

Courtesy of The Pictorial Studio, Newcastle

tours, bottling demonstrations, and, of course, plenty of free samples. What also stands out in Win's memory is that all the employees wore uniforms for the occasion: "You didn't just go to work in coveralls or your usual work clothes *that* day."

Painted
label bottle,
1961

Crystal Bottling Company
Biddeford

From Greece (where he was born in 1890) to Montreal (where he immigrated in 1917) to Biddeford (where he settled in 1923): that's a capsule account of the life of Dennis Vanites, the founder of Crystal Bottling.

Dennis' son, Jim, recalls that his dad came to Canada to seek his success. But it was in Biddeford that he found it. After six years of working numerous jobs in Montreal, Dennis heard that the Hanscom Bottling Company in Biddeford could be bought. He bought it.

From 1923 to 1929, Dennis operated his company, renamed Crystal Bottling, out of the for-

Courtesy of Rick Poore, Standish

Photo, circa 1934. That's Dennis in the center; Jim's uncle, Andrew, to the right; Jim's brother, Theodore, perched on the truck. The man on the left is unidentified. I especially love one of the stories Jim told me about his dad. Seems that, on nice summer Sundays back in 1937-1941, Dennis would take two or three of his trucks, turn soda cases into seats, load up parishioners from the Greek Orthodox church on Emery Street, and take them all for an outing at Goose Rocks Beach. "After church, of course," he quickly adds.

mer Hanscom plant at 419-421 Main Street, then moved to larger quarters at 310 Alfred Street. In addition to distributing Moxie, he bottled a very full line of - as his ads phrased it - "high grade tonics." Strawberry, black raspberry, peach, lemon blossom, ginger ale, birch beer, etc., etc: Crystal had them all. Plus the company had a taste-tester supreme: Jim well remembers that his dad would bring home a sampling of just-bottled flavors each day at lunch and that his mother, Georgia, would dutifully partake of each. If they weren't completely right she'd announce it in no uncertain terms. "Too much syrup or too much carbonation," she'd say.

After World War II, as competion from the national giants really heated up, Dennis began adding franchised brands to his own Crystal line. Hire's Root Beer was first, followed by Squirt, NuGrape, Nesbit, and Triple Cola. But it was a losing battle. As Jim, who worked at the bottling plant from age 13 on, says: "The big boys just kept getting bigger." Plus his dad was not getting any younger. Father and son began selling the business in bits and pieces in 1965. By 1966 Crystal Bottling was no more.

Dennis Vanites passed away in February, 1968. Jim still resides in Biddeford, where he's a broker for Spartan Realty. Their former

bottling works on Alfred Street is now home to Atlantic Coffee & Snack Service. Considerably enlarged in 1937-1938, it little resembles the rather jaunty false-front building pictured here.

Business card, circa 1950

Crystal Lake Kabins
Gray

Crystal Lake Kabins started out as Crystal Lake Villa, with Arthur Wilson as proprietor, in 1930. In 1938, the property was purchased by Richard Green, who owned it until 1947 or so, and who maintained the Villa name. Next proprietor in line was Ernest Phalen. It was he who made the change to Crystal Lake Kabins. One final name change was made in 1957, to Crystal Lake Motor Court and Restaurant. In the early 1960s Phalen sold out to Philip Humphrey, who converted the restaurant to a saddle and leather store. Humphrey kept things going until the early 1970s. He then

shuttered the almost half-century-old wayside rest.

What's nice is that the Crystal Lake is not unlike a family that's grown up: it's scattered but yet pretty much intact. The former restaurant, a winsome maroon structure, sits on cement blocks on the left side of Route 26 coming into Poland Village from the south. And the cabins? Well, they're scattered here and there and everywhere in the Gray/New Gloucester/Poland area. At least three of them, however, are still unsettled...and for sale. As a result, you may buy one (or all three!) of them. Just stop in at Buddy's Store, Route 26, New Gloucester. Ask for Buddy.

Labels, circa 1935. While ginger ale was always Crystal Spring's top seller it got a run for its money in the late 1950s. The challenger was white cream. It turns out, Richard told me, that cream soda is, of its own accord, white in color. For some

reason, bottlers traditionally add food coloring to create the brownish hue so familiar to all of us. Well, one day around 1958 Richard's uncle, Meyer, was making a batch of cream soda when he noticed he was out of brown food coloring. "The heck with it," he decided, "I'll put it out as it is." The customers loved it! Smiles Richard: "It became a hit by accident."

Courtesy of Dianne and Richard Bornstein, Auburn

Crystal Spring Beverage Company
Auburn

It's a melodramatic story. But it's a true story. Crystal clear spring water flows down the parched throats of thousands of thirsty Mainers (I said it was melodramatic!) each and every day because of the simple utterance of a willful woman 90-odd years ago. The utterance: "I'll marry you. But I won't move to Rumford."

But let's back up a bit. To 1880. That was the year Louis Borenstein was born in Kiev, Russia. At age 19, in 1899, he immigrated to the United States and, because he had an uncle living there, he settled in Rumford. Circa 1905 his uncle arranged a marriage for Louis. The intended was Marsha Alpharin (also spelled Alpren). She said "yes," but then appended the always and forever "but I won't move" words. Marsha lived in Auburn and she liked it. So Louis moved to Auburn.

In Rumford, Louis had been a junk dealer. In the Twin Cities he pursued the same occupation, setting up shop on Lincoln Street in Lewiston. Next door, by chance, was a small bottling works, the Maine Bottling Company. In 1911 or thereabouts Louis decided it was time to change direction: he bought the bottling business and got out of the junk business. Somewhere along the way he also changed

his name to Lewis Bornstein.

All went well in the soda business with one exception: Lewis had to pay for his water and he thought he was paying too much. As a result, when he heard that a natural spring - operated by the Auburn Crystal Spring Company - in Auburn was for sale, he upped and purchased it. That would've been about 1915. But his bottling operation remained in Lewiston, at 216-218 Lincoln, and his company's name remained the Maine Bottling Company (later also known as the Maine and Rumford Bottling Company). Lewis would cart his water from the spring to Lincoln Street and there he'd process and blend it into soda.

Richard Bornstein, Lewis' grandson, recalls that Lewis really loved the soda business. He especially enjoyed the blending and mixing involved in the making of the different flavors: "He used to go to the drug store and buy his ginger root and his extracts and then make the soda himself." Lewis Bornstein was a real soda maker. Plus he loved to drink soda. "He'd drink it all day long," Richard smiles as he reminisces. His favorite was his Gold Bond (there was gold foil wrapped around the neck of every bottle) Ginger Ale.

In the early 1930s Lewis decided it was time to quit hauling water from Auburn to Lewiston. He

and five of his children constructed, with their own hands, the impressive brick building on Washington Avenue in Auburn that remains Crystal Spring's headquarters to this day. Lewis made the move to the new building - which sits conveniently atop the spring - circa 1935.

Lewis' soda business remained strong all the days of his life. In addition to his own full line of Crystal Spring/Gold Bond flavors he, at one time or another, bottled under franchise such national brands as Hires, Whistle, Coca-Cola, Mission Orange, Fruit Bowl, Big Giant Cola, and Lemmy Lemonade. Lewis, around 1936, could even have had the local Pepsi-Cola franchise. But he didn't want it. "There's no way I'm going to give them (customers) 12 ounces for a nickel," he is reputed to have said to the man who had called on him.

Lewis Bornstein passed away December 31, 1962. He was 82. And he'd seen the American Dream - work hard and ye shall succeed - come true.

Lewis' son, Rudolph, took over upon his father's death. Nicknamed "Sonny," he guided the company until he, too, passed away, in January of 1981. It was during his tenure that Crystal Spring got into the bottled water business. Circa 1970 Rudolph bought out a longtime Lewiston/Auburn rival, the Highland

Golden ORANGE Refreshment

Advertising sign, 1951. Whistle was one of a number of nationally-franchised brands bottled and locally distributed by Crystal Spring. Richard Bornstein recalls enjoying it as a youngster; that it was an orange soda that was "different than the others." It was originated by a man named Sylvester Jones in Columbus, Ohio in 1916. And - surprise! - it's still made. The rights today are held by Vess Beverages of Maryland Heights, Missouri, and it's sold in 30 states, mostly in the midwest. I asked Don Schneeberger, president of Vess, if he still used the drink's famous "Thirsty? Just Whistle" slogan. He laughed and replied "Sure."

Spring Bottling Company. Highland Spring had a small number of bottled water customers. Rudolph, to be obliging, continued to service those customers.

Enter the third generation. Richard Bornstein was born in Auburn in 1943. He graduated from Edward Little in 1962 and from Mid-State College in 1966. Along the way, not surprisingly, he was introduced to the bottling business. "I started at the very top," he chuckles, "sorting bottles and sweeping floors and the like." That was 1956, when Richard was 13. Today, at 51, he oversees a most successful operation. But it's a bottled water operation; not a soda pop operation. "My life in the bottling business," he states unequivocally, "didn't get good until we got in the water business." That happened in a full-fledged way in 1980. As Richard relates it: "That was a very, very bad year. Coca-Cola decided they didn't want any other soda companies in business and they gave a cooler to all stores that would carry only Coke and Fanta. So we kept losing customers."

It was, as it turns out, actually a blessing. "We were phasing out of the soda and into water anyway," Richard confesses. Crystal Spring ceased soda production in August of 1980. In the years since things haven't been all milk and honey, but they have been very good. When I spoke with Richard in January of 1995

Photo, January 1995, showing Richard and a small part of the tribute to sodas gone-by that he's created inside his building. It's almost like a Soda Pop Museum.

Photo, January 1995. Crystal Spring's good-looking headquarters are located between the old and the new Washington Avenue. The old road is now named Brickyard Circle. It used to be named Crystal Spring Curve. Richard feels that it still should be.
The building was constructed by Lewis Bornstein and his family in the early 1930s. But it looks to be much older. And that's a compliment.
The "Est. 1855" comes by way of a title search that indicated Crystal Spring water has been bottled continuously by someone or other as least as far back as 1855.

he admitted that the big boom in the water business occurred in the late 1980s, and that business dropped in the early 1990s. But he senses that the market is coming back strong again.

Including Richard's brothers, Bob, 47, and Peter, 45 (who are co-proprietors of Crystal Spring) and his wife, Dianne, 46, ("She really runs the company," laughs Richard), Crystal Spring employs 15 people and nine trucks. Their big five-gallon bottles are distributed from Pittsfield to Kittery. Is there a fourth generation waiting in the wings? "Not yet," answers Richard. "They (daughter Stephanie, 23, and son Jacob, 20) haven't gotten out in the real world yet." Neither, obviously, has Peter's daughter, Natalie, aged two. But Richard's hoping one or more develop the desire. As he once summed up the water business in an article in the Lewiston *Sunday Sun Journal*: "You work hard, but you feel good about what you're doing."

41

The Dodge Inn
Edgecomb

Two years into the Depression, in 1931, brothers Irving and Moses Davis decided to take a risk. They built a restaurant. They chose their site well: on the banks of the Sheepscot River just across from Wiscasset. Local residents Gus and Helen Lewis liked what they saw and they decided to take a risk, too. They leased the restaurant. They selected a rather evocative name, the Lewis Spa, and ran it successfully until 1936, when Gus passed away. Helen, however, persevered. By herself, and later with her second husband, Walter Boynton, she kept the restaurant very much in operation until 1947. Then, feeling the effects of age, she sold to Stan

Circa 1965 postcard views.
Courtesy of Marj and Mel Johnson, Hartford, Connecticut.

and Velma Dodge of Wiscasset, who changed the restaurant's name to the Dodge Inn.

Eighty-one year old Laurence

Davis, son of Irving, recalls the Dodge Inn well...that it specialized in seafood and steaks and that it was very popular: "They were open at 11:30 AM and the dining room would be filled up in no time and people would be waiting in line."

After almost three decades the Dodges decided to say goodbye to the restaurant business in 1976. They operated as a gift shop in 1977. The Inn then sat idle until 1980 when it was reopened, as the Muddy Rudder, by Charlie Keegan. Keegan, a Wisconsin native, had been successful with his first Muddy Rudder in Yarmouth and figured Maine was ready for another. He was right. Muddy Rudder II - if you will - was so successful that Keegan razed it in 1989 in order to both expand and to overcome what manager Deb Sondergaard describes as "a rickety foundation." You might, then, call the present-day structure Muddy Rudder III. In any case, it is no longer affiliated with its Yarmouth cousin. Of greater importance is the fact that the site on which the restaurant stands, selected by Irving and Moses Davis over six decades ago, is still a delight.

Dowe's Lakeview Tea Room

SODAS   LUNCHES   ICE CREAM

Try our Hamburg Sandwiches
The best you've ever had
They put a smile upon your face
And make your stomach glad

TEL. SO. CHINA 31–2   So. CHINA, MAINE

Dowe's Lakeview Tea Room
South China

Opened in the early 1930s, Dowe's Lakeview Tea Room was the apex of a small Dowe's "empire" that at one time or another included a dance pavilion, diner, and overnight cabins. Proprietors Alice and Ed Dowe were noted for their hamburgers, fried clams, ice cream, doughnuts, pies...and an occasional good corny rhyme. The Tea Room closed in the late 1960s. Its former site at the corner of old Route 3 and Town Landing Road is now occupied by a storage building.

Dreamland Theatre
Livermore Falls

The Dreamland began in a rather undreamylike way: as a no-name stable-come-theatre where early one-reelers were shown for the price of 5¢ admission. Known briefly as the Star Theatre in 1908-1909, it became the Dreamland in 1909-1910. At the time it was one of but four theatres in Androscoggin County; the only one outside of Lewiston.

In the 1920s the Dreamland became part of Maine-New Hampshire Theatres, Inc. Joe Langlais, later Dreamland manager, recalls that's when the theatre did actually become "dreamy": an interior decorator was hired and "paid a fortune" to spiff things up. Joe, unfortunately, has even better recall of the theatre's decline. He was manager from 1956 to 1961; had the not-very-pleasant task of closing the venerable structure in October, 1961. "It was sad," he says simply. The building was razed in 1966-1967. Its former site on Main Street is today a parking lot.

Ad, April 1939. For most of its life the Dreamland was part of Maine-New Hampshire Theatres, Inc., a chain owned by none other than Joe Kennedy.

Dreamland Theatre, Livermore Falls, Me.

Postcard view, circa 1930   Courtesy of Maine Historic Preservation Commission, Augusta

Empire Theatre, Lewiston, Me.

Empire Theatre
Lewiston

"You went down to the Empire in Lewiston if you *really* wanted to go to the movies." So states Gary Knight, 51, of Livermore Falls. That's because the Empire was the most lavish, the most spectacular, theatre in south central Maine. It was a palace...and it always will be to all who recall it in its heyday.

To Claire Ward, 52, of Lewiston, the Empire was "a classy place...beautiful, with velvet seats, a huge curtain, and the 'nicer' films. It was," she sums up, "where you'd go on a date with your beau." To Margaret Dunlap, 74, of Auburn, the Empire was "quite grand." Margaret especially enjoyed going to see Nelson Eddy/Jeanette Mac-Donald movies. "I was just a romantic kid," she laughs.

A person who recalls the Empire especially well is Kenneth Conner. And well he should: he served as the theatre's manager for a remarkable 35 years, from 1929 to 1964. Now 91, Ken describes the Empire as "very much in the opera house style...very ornate...with plush trimmings." What he perhaps recalls most, though, is the huge stage the theatre possessed up to 1940. "It was so big you could've had a Ben Hur chariot race on it," he states dramatically. And then, to prove his point, he continues: "In fact, they actually did have a chariot race on that stage once, with horses and everything." Ken's memory recalls that it was right around 1910, as part of a spectacle entitled *The First Crusade*.

One other memory involves my wife, Catherine Buotte. She tells the story of her Great Aunt Tess.

Tess had just moved from rural New Brunswick to Maine and had never seen a talking picture. That was to change one day in the early 1930s. As Buotte family legend has it: "Tess and my grandmother and my mother went to this movie - at the Empire - and the bad guy was trying to seduce the young, innocent heroine and at one point they were going to kiss and my great-aunt stood up and yelled out, 'No, don't do it'...much to my mother's mortification."

The Empire opened to great fanfare on November 23, 1903. "Magnificent;" "massive;" "sumptous": those were the words sung by the press. The theatre's entrance was described as "noble;" its lobby as "Pompeian;" its color scheme as "old rose blended into salmon." Mahogany and brass and stained glass abounded. Seven-hundred thousand bricks were used in the theatre's construction. And its name came from its design in the Empire style...the style of architecture in vogue during the reign of Napoleon.

The Empire slowly evolved from a stage house to a movie house. A 1927 ad reads: "You may rest assured that the great pictures of the times are on their way to the Empire," further extolling the theatre as "The House That Has The Pictures."

In 1940 the Empire was com-

44

pletely remodeled. Gone were the theatre's double balconies (The second balcony had long been nicknamed "Angel's Paradise"!), replaced by a single one. In were new seats, all new sound equipment, and a new ventilating system. Remaining was the theatre's beauty. In fact, a *Lewiston Sun* reporter of the day wrote: "The new theatre is better looking, more comfortable and more convenient."

Modern times - especially cable TV - eventually caught up with the Empire, of course. By the early 1980s patrons were few. It was time to call it quits. And that's just what proprietor G. Raymond Cailler did. The grand old theatre's last show was in April of 1982.

After its long run as a theatre, the Empire served as a house of worship. From 1984 to 1993 it was home to the Christian Family Church. Since 1983 it's been owned by Tom Platz, head of the Auburn architectural firm of Platz Associates. Tom is 43, a Lewiston/Auburn native, and an Empire devotee. He'd clearly love to see the theatre restored, but admits to not having "outlined a particular plan to accomplish that." Given Tom's involvement with the successful restoration of the crosstown Ritz Theatre (included in *Good Old Maine*), though, I suspect there's a better than even chance the Empire will be born again, too. A lot of people would like that.

Ads from through the years. The Empire was known for showing what Kenneth Conner calls the "A" pictures... "the best pictures." "We," he states with more than just a little pride, "had the Garbos, the Clark Gables, the Katherine Hepburns."

1918

1939

The Empire traditionally showed but one movie. A single feature! Let the Strand, the Priscilla, and the Ritz show two: when you had the big films all you needed was one!

1948

Ernie's Drive-In
Brunswick

Before there was McDonald's and Burger King and all the rest there was Ernie's. Ernie's #1 was born in Farmingdale in 1944 (please see page 65). Ernie's #2 began in Brunswick in 1949. Ernie's #3 started in Auburn in 1956. It's #2 that we're interested in here. And it really should have been called "Herb's" instead of "Ernie's".

It was 1949. Gardiner High grad Herb Thulen, 21, was finishing his three years of study at Bentley College in Boston. Ernie's in Farmingdale was enjoying its

Photo, 1949. Ernie's when it was young and reckless and at its first Brunswick location.

Courtesy of Herb Thulen, Brunswick

Menu cover, circa 1950. Hot dogs were 15¢; hamburgers were 20¢; and, if you really wanted to splurge, a chicken dinner was $1.00.

Courtesy of Herb Thulen, Brunswick

fifth season of success. And Herb and older brother Ernie decided it was time to try a second drive-in. They opened in May at 42 Bath Road, where the Chuck Wagon Restaurant is now. It was called Ernie's because, as Herb explains with obvious brotherly pride, "Ernie was the moving force behind all the drive-ins."

Carhops were a fixture from the very first day. Actually, they were an absolute neccessity: there just wasn't enough space in the eat-in section to handle the carloads of customers that showed up. In fact, in an extensive August 1994 interview with Herb and his wife and aide-de-camp Charlotte, it became readily apparent that being a "father" and "grand-

FOR DELICIOUS FOOD!
Drive-In GOOD SERVICE!

ERNIE'S
ROUTE 201 - GARDINER
ROUTE 1 - BRUNSWICK

father" to the literally hundreds of carhops he employed over the years is very meaningful to Herb. He's proud that he had several cases of three generation carhops: grandmother, mother, daughter. He's also proud that, by his estimate, at least half of his carhops met their future husband while working at Ernie's. "And most of them are still married," he adds!

In 1958, Herb was forced to make a change of address. He was leasing the site at 42 Bath Road. The owners wanted to sell the land and gave Herb the right of first refusal. But Herb and Charlotte couldn't come up with the necessary money, and so decided to move operations down the road to 18 Bath, to a site they already owned. Their new place - which is still today's

place - was constructed in late 1958 and opened in February/March of 1959.

It was at the new location that Herb and Charlotte enjoyed their best years. That was in the sixties. "The sixties, definitely the sixties," Herb says flat out. He credits that to both he and his staff being better organized...better able to serve whatever hungry hoards appeared on

Ad, July 1964. It was a good year: Ernie's in Farmingdale celebrated its 20th birthday; Ernie's in Brunswick its 15th.

Courtesy of Herb Thulen, Brunswick

Photo, August 1994. Carhop Danielle Withers, 18, of Bowdoinham takes an order. I asked Danielle what she liked best about carhopping in ten words or less. She came in at nine: "You get to be outside. It's fun. It's easy."

Photo, August 1994. Gail and Roger in front of Ernie's original 1949 neon sign and their 1966 Olds Delta 88. The neon - a real beauty! - came with the restaurant. The Delta 88 was "new": they purchased it in June to go along with the drive-in's motif.

the scene. That especially paid off on Fridays: "We used to do a wicked business on Fridays," Herb and Charlotte both well recall.

By 1989 the day-in day-out wear and tear had gotten to Herb. He had serious knee problems, and Charlotte and their son Greg convinced him that it was time to retire. The drive-in sat idle through the 1989 and 1990 seasons. Herb then leased it to Bill Keller, who also owned a wholesale seafood business. It proved to be too much. Bill ran the drive-in through 1993 and then called it quits.

Ernie's keeps bouncing back, however. In early 1994, Gail and Roger Riendeau, both 42 and both Brunswick natives, decided they wanted to keep Ernie's and its tradition alive. The Grand Reopening was May 19! When I spoke with Gail and Roger in August they were delighted at how well things were going. Herb's happy, too, beaming: "They keep the drive-in the way we used to...neat as a pin." Happiest of all, though, are the customers: they're glad to be able to get back to such Ernie's favorites as clams and batter, onions and batter, and those famous Canadian bacon 3Ds!

Fairyland Theatre
Camden

Fairyland was the creation of a Mr. A.D. Foudry. He had the theatre constructed in the winter of 1907-1908, and opened it on March 13, 1908. "The Latest Moving Pictures and Illustrated Songs" were promised. Admission was 10¢ for adults, 5¢ for children. "Mechanic Street," in the theatre's inaugural ad, somehow came out being spelled "Chanic Street."

The theatre was well received. The *Camden Herald* of March 20th reported "Everybody is going to Fairyland this week," and in the March 27th issue it was written "And still the crowds move toward Fairyland."

Crowds or not, Fairyland saw numerous changes in ownership: it changed hands four times in its five years of existence as a theatre. The final proprietor was Sophus Hansen. Hansen, who'd made good as a baker in Camden, had big plans in store for local moviegoers. In January of 1913 he added almost 200 additional seats, laid a new floor, and constructed an orchestra pit. It wasn't enough. Again, the *Camden Herald*: "Soon after Sophus Hansen bought out the Fairyland Theatre he found that what was needed here was a theatre larger than Fairyland and with modern and up-to-date conveniences." Hansen began work on such a theatre in April 1913. And, in

keeping with Mechanic Street and movies going so well together, he built this new theatre right next door to Fairyland. Hansen's new entertainment hub, named the Comique Theatre, opened on July 23, 1913. Its coming signaled Fairyland's going.

Over eight decades after it ceased being a theatre, the former Fairyland building at 6 Mechanic Street is yet going strong. It is now home to French & Brawn Home Baked Goods. Its neighbor at 10 Mechanic Street survives nicely, too. What was the Comique and later the Camden Theatre has been converted to the Camden Store.

It was formal portrait time in this photo, circa 1910. Today, eight and a half decades later, the outside of the former theatre looks remarkably as it does here.

49

Flo's Hot Dogs
Cape Neddick

You don't go to Flo's for fried clams. Or steak. Or ham and eggs. You go to Flo's for steamed hot dogs smothered in a secret hot sauce. You go for the taste. And you won't be disappointed.

What is today Flo's began as a very small hot dog stand, owned by Bob Johnson, in 1947. After a decade Bob sold to Al and Anne Duchaine. They called it Anne's, but only operated for one year, 1958. Then entered the woman who became a Route 1 legend, Flo Stacy. Flo, 51 years old at the time, was a native of Mercer, Maine and a former schoolteacher. What set her apart was her sauce and her "cantankerousness." She doesn't really, however, take credit for the sauce. "I bought it with the business," she says. (Although "I 'titillated' it a little," she adds). But she does take credit for

Photo, March 1994. Rick Merrill, Arundel, Bill Boston, Wells, and Mike Burgess, Kennebunkport, enjoy their hot dogs beneath the pale blue sky in Flo's parking lot. Flo's is open year-around daily except Wednesday from 11:00 AM to 3:00 PM.

Photo. August 1994. Same sauce, less sass: Gail adds a smile to an outgoing order of steamed dogs.

being cantankerous. "I'm a very outspoken person," she says right off. "When I was behind the counter I was boss." Flo would go after patrons with a broom or lock them out if they misbehaved. "It's a wonder I had any customers at all," she laughs.

In 1973 Flo sold the business to her son and daughter-in-law, John and Gail Stacy, who have kept Flo's pretty much as it was. The menu is basic: coffee, milk, soda, chips, and, of course, hot dogs. The building is basic, too.

"Unornate" might be a better word. It's one story and brown on the outside. Inside there's the kitchen, the counter, six stools, and a small standing area, all wedged under a ceiling so low it would make Mickey Rooney feel like a giant. Mostly, though, there's the same secret sauce. The story goes that Heinz came and tried to buy the recipe and Flo told them "to go to hell." When they persisted, asking her what she put in it that makes it so special, she replied "If I'm in a bad mood I put in a lot of sass."

Fossett's Ice Cream Bar
Union

It was 1936 and the Depression had settled in and Harold Fossett decided that what Union needed was an ice cream shoppe. Featuring cones and sundaes and frappes, Fossett's Ice Cream Bar delighted many a sweet tooth from 1936 to 1946. As 66-year old Union native Mary Carver fondly recalls: "It was a local hangout for the kids of Union High School. We used to come down from school on noon hour. And," she only now admits, "sometimes we didn't make it back on time."

Actually, though, by the time Mary graduated - she was class of 1946 - Harold Fossett had pretty much had it with the ice cream business. The war years, with its sugar rationing, had not been especially kind. Plus he was a successful insurance agent. He sold out to Elmer Goff in 1946. Elmer - probably far better known for his Elmer's Restaurant (now the Eastside), founded in 1962 - operated the shop as E.F. Goff Ice Cream Bar and Drug Store into the seventies, until 1972.

Harold Fossett, recalled as "a really nice person." died circa 1955. Elmer Goff is still very much alive and well and living in Union. The shop where they both dished out sundaes and scoops and cones is now occupied by a video store.

Postcard view, circa 1940. Built in 1895 by H.L. Robbins, the building to the right has always and forever been known as the Robbins Block, while the building on the left is the Odd Fellows' building. Things don't look all that different today. Only the occupants have changed. Now, left to right, there's a Norge Laundry and Cleaning Village, Hannibal's Cafe, Oakside Video, and Cricket Gift Store.

Frey's Cafe
Bangor

Charles H. Frey could have been called "Mr. Central Street." Born in Bangor in 1866, he began his restaurant career as a waiter at age 14 at Charles Aiken's restaurant on Central Street, progressed to clerk at C.H. Buswell's restaurant on Central Street and, at 24, opened his own place in 1890. On Central Street, of course. At first he was at 18 Central. By 1895, however, he was rolling at the location he'd make a landmark, 28-30 Central.

Frey's had several dining areas. There was a lunch room on the street floor, with formal dining rooms - including one reserved for ladies only - on the second. The kitchen was on the third. Meals were served at all hours. A 1919 ad promised "high class chefs on duty every hour in the 24." Specialties were chops, steak, and lobster.

Even Bangor's Great Fire of 1911 did not daunt Charles Frey. He and his brother William, a partner since 1901, rebuilt on the same site, taking great pains to ensure that the new Frey's was even more gracious than the original.

Charles Frey sold his restaurant and retired in January of 1927. He died a little over a year later, in March of 1928. In its obituary, the *Bangor Daily News* described Charles Frey as "kindly, genial...never relaxing his interest in giving the best possible public service."

What's nice about Frey's is that, all these years later, much of its graciousness survives. Walk into Alcott Antiques, 30 Central Street, and admire. When Patricia Alcott purchased what is now her antique shop in 1986 things were pretty rough. The former restaurant had been through many hands since its days as Frey's. But as Patricia and her daughter Sasha started to uncover things they noticed that a lot of the original detail was still there. The more they dug the more they found. "It was extremely exciting...because we discovered all this original stuff," reports Patricia. Tin ceilings, tin walls, tile flooring: these are a few of Patricia's favorite things. It's easy to see why.

1917

Why Not Eat at FREY'S CAFE ?

The most up-to-date SANITARY CAFE in the State of Maine.
Dining Room for Ladies and Gentlemen up-stairs.
We will try and merit your Patronage.

JUST TRY US.

BROILED LIVE LOBSTERS A SPECIALTY.

FREY'S LEADING CAFE

MEALS AT ALL HOURS   Bangor, Maine

c. 1905

30 and 32 Central St.,

FREY'S CAFE

OPEN
ALL NIGHT

28-30 Central St.

IS A FAVORITE
AMONG THE
COLLEGE
MEN

Bangor

Ads, circa 1905-1917. In addition to its food and service, Frey's was noted for being a prolific advertiser... and for its cleanliness. Charles Frey was a stickler when it came to matters of sanitation. So much so, in fact, that he often designated his restaurant as Frey's Sanitary Cafe in his ads.

We Will Please You

When you are in Bangor and want to get a nice dinner or lunch in an up to date Cafe, we can please you. We handle the best the market affords and have Chefs that know how to cook it. Cleanliness and pure foods are our motto. We furnish waiters to serve you and our prices are reasonable. We want your patronage.

FREY'S SANITARY CAFE

30-32 CENTRAL STREET   BANGOR, MAINE

1916

Fryeburg Dairy Milk and Ice Cream Bar
Fryeburg

Fryeburg Dairy, which had been in business since the 1920s, added a new dimension to the joys of summer when it opened its Milk and Ice Cream Bar in 1936 or so. The dairy's Fryeburg Dairymaide Ice Cream still draws rave reviews from those old enough to remember it. "It was good, rich ice cream," recalls 68-year old Gerald Kiesman, whose favorite flavor was strawberry. Sixty-five-year old Bub Osgood liked the cones: "I remember it was a nickel for a single scoop, 10¢ for the big double." Bub's favorites were chocolate and, quite exotic for its time, orange pineapple.

Fryeburg Dairy was purchased by H.P. Hood and Sons around 1943. Hood closed the Milk and Ice Cream Bar in order to concentrate on the milk processing plant, which it operated until circa 1950.

The building pictured here, located on Bridgton Road/Route 302 East directly across from the Jockey Cap Motel and Cabins, is still in existence. But you'd never recognize it. It is today home to the Jockey Cap Laundromat.

Calendar, 1941

53

Gayety Theatre
Van Buren

A theatre known as the Dreamland Opera House opened behind an existing general store at 48-54 Main Street in the heart of Van Buren in 1912. It was the start of over seven decades of movie tradition at that address. The Dreamland burned in January 1920. The general store did, too. The result was the construction of a brand new theatre-only building. It was named the Star Theatre. Alas, though, fire struck again in December of 1924, necessitating almost complete reconstruction. When the theatre reopened in mid-1925 it was still the Star. But not for long. A husband and wife team, Lillian and Harold Keegan, took over management in August of the same year. They renamed it the Gayety.

As the Gayety, the theatre served Van Buren moviegoers for 58

years, until 1983. Its heyday came in the 1940s and 1950s. The theatre sold about 250,000 tickets in both decades... enough to earn Lillian - sole proprietor after Harold died in 1950 - the title of "The Aroostook Millionaire."

Lillian Keegan sold the theatre in March of 1961. It then changed hands two more times within a year before Gilman Grandmaison purchased it in March 1962. Dayton Grandmaison, Gilman's son, characterizes his dad's first ten years in the movie business as "good," the next five as "pretty good," and the remainder as "bad." "After the late 1970s it was all downhill fast," he sums up, blaming the decline on a combination of fewer residents and more television.

The last show was December 4, 1983. The building then sat vacant until 1988, when Dayton bought it from his father. Dayton, who's 28 and who grew up in awe of the theatre, confesses he would have loved to reopen it as a movie house. "It's a wonderful idea," he laughs, "but nobody would come." Instead he converted the building to a restaurant and named it Dayton's. He's very proud, though, that much of the Gayety survives: original clocks, posters and lobby cards, chrome lights, tin ceiling, and front door handles. Of greater importance, however, is the building's facade: it may say "Dayton's Restaurant" but it looks like "Gayety Theatre." And that's good.

Photo, September 1994

Governor's
Stillwater

There are no early photos of Governor's reproduced on this page for good reason. Governor's co-propieters Leith and Donna Wadleigh didn't take any. "We felt there was not much chance we'd make it," Leith laughs now, "and we didn't want photos around as a reminder of failure."

As with so many ventures, Governor's didn't just happen. It evolved. It started as a tiny take-out-only ice cream stand named Cree-Mee's. Even that evolved. Leith had graduated from Old Town High in 1955. His father wanted him to be a doctor, and Leith dutifully enrolled at UMO. He hated it. "Organic Chemistry and I just did not get along," Leith freely admits. In 1958, Leith dropped out, preferring to work in his dad's general store.

Then fortune smiled. Next to the general store was a field, occupied only by a few cabins from when his father had operated a cabin court. When Leith pondered opening an ice cream stand, his dad suggested he take one of the cabins and "see what you can do." So, in June of 1960, Cree-Mee's was launched. It was a joint venture: Leith had married his high-school sweetheart, Donna, in 1957. The original plan was to operate all year long... "but then October and November arrived and nobody came anymore."

After again being open for the summer only in 1961, Leith and Donna splurged and bought a used grill for $100.00 in early 1962. "I commenced to cook," Leith laughs again. It was a smart move: Leith and Donna sold enough food to add an inside counter and to remain open all year around. A name change appeared in order, too. "Governor's" came about because Leith had a problem common to a lot of people. He couldn't remember people's names. He called everyone "Governor." So Governor's it became.

Twenty or so additions later, Governor's is still Governor's. Plus, in addition to the original Governor's on Route 2A in Stillwater, there are now satellite Governor's in Bangor, Westbrook, and Waterville. Total sales in 1993 were $8,000,000 (up $7,992,000 from 1960!). Leith and Donna's son and co-proprietor, Randy, 31, credits the restaurant's success to good homemade cooking and a constant array of different daily specials. And that "My parents killed themselves working night and day for years." Leith has his views, too. He credits the ever changing nature of the food business with keeping him, personally, going: the new additions, the new equipment, the constant changes in the menu. And of course, Donna: "Without her I'd probably be working in a mill somewhere."

Menu illustration, 1994. The Governor's symbol is, appropriately, a rather jaunty fellow nicknamed the Governor. Modeled after New York's infamous Boss Tweed, the Governor is seemingly everywhere in the restaurant... on its signs, its walls, its menu. In days of old he perpetually had a cigar in his hand or in his mouth. Now he's less apt to. "Public relations, you know," explained Randy.

55

Graphic Theatre
Bangor

The Graphic is very largely forgotten now, but it was a theatre of note for almost two decades. And when it opened in February of 1909 you'd have thought it was the event of the decade. "This is winter, and a savage winter at that - deep snow, icy sidewalks, and the mercury near zero, but the people came out, just as if were balmy May," emoted the *Bangor Daily News*. "The opening had been announced for seven o'clock, and long before that time the entrance to the theatre was surrounded by a crowd numbering hundreds. At 7:15 every one of

the 900 seats had been taken, and still the crowd kept coming, until at 7:30 the standing room was full, likewise the foyer and the lobby, with an overflow to the sidewalk." Summed up the paper: "All the four-leaved clovers, rabbits' feet and horseshoes in the world couldn't have brought more good luck to the new Graphic Theatre than it had

on its opening night."

The Graphic - which was described as possessing a "brilliant lobby and foyer, spacious auditorium, and all the comforts and conveniences" - was launched by a former travelling salesman named Haven Grant and a former bottler named John Burns. They owned and operated the theatre until 1918 when successful businessman Edwin Epstein became proprietor. Local clothier Samuel Kurson was the Graphic's last proprietor, from April 1926 (when Epstein died) to April 1927. Both Epstein and Kurson also headed the Graphic Circuit, a Bangor-based company that controlled theatres throughout northern New England, and it was presumably the success of this endeavor that allowed Kurson to forego operation of the chain's flagship. The Graphic's last show was a boxing melodrama entitled *His Rise to Fame* on April 2, 1927.

The theatre's former site at 177 Exchange Street is now occupied by a parking lot for Maliseet Gardens Plaza, and a newish building most recently home to Paine Webber.

EXCHANGE STREET, BANGOR, MAINE   95226

Postcard view, circa 1920. When the Graphic, shown here to the left, opened to an overflow crowd on February 18, 1909, the *Bangor Daily News* wrote: "People who saw the crush say that it's about time to change the name of Exchange Street to 42nd, for it reminded them of that famous theatre region of New York."
Today there is not so much as a single trace of so much as a single building shown in this view. They're all gone.
Courtesy of the Maine Historic Preservation Commission.

Green Moors
Kittery

When it opened circa 1922 the Green Moors was set on a tract of land almost universally characterized as "poor" and "barren." Somehow "green moors" sounded pretty good by comparison.

The roadside restaurant's founder was Charles S. Higgins. In the early 1930s he sold it to William O. Dixon of Laconia, New Hampshire, who operated it until the late 1930s. While I found several people who clearly remembered the Green Moors, I found few who'd actually eaten there. As lifelong resident Effie Phillips, 68, explained: "The Green Moors was not a place where people in school or just out of school would have gone to. It was out of our price range!" A person who did dine at the Green Moors is 91-year old Anna M. Young, also a lifelong Kittery resident. In fact she ate there quite a few times. She recalls the decor as "lovely," the food as "excellent," and the shore dinner as especially excellent.

During the 1940s the restaurant was reopened as Warren's Star Dust Inn by Warren "Pete" Wurm, founder of the well-known - and still in business - Warren's Lobster House. It later became just plain Stardust and then, beginning in 1960, was home to the Dragon Seed Chinese Restaurant, until demol-

GREEN MOORS INN, ON STATE ROAD BETWEEN PORTSMOUTH, N. H. AND YORK, MAINE

A SPECIAL CHICKEN DINNER IS ALSO SERVED

GREEN MOORS' FAMOUS SHORE DINNER ACCLAIMED BEST IN NEW ENGLAND

ished by fire circa 1975. On the site today is Harve Benard and FAO Schwarz, two of the shops that make up what somebody named Manufacturer's Outlet Mall.

GREEN MOORS INN, ON STATE ROAD BETWEEN PORTSMOUTH, N. H., AND YORK, MAINE.

THE BEST LOBSTER AND CLAM DINNER IN NEW ENGLAND.

57

The Green Moth
Trenton

Legend has it that a large Luna moth - that's the one with green wings - landed near workers during the construction of a grocery store/luncheonette one day around 1928. The man responsible for the building's construction, Bar Harbor native and proprietor Bill Schlotzhauer, must have considered it an omen: he christened his endeavor the Green Moth. Not only that, but Schlotzhauer loved baseball, fielding a team in the strong semi-pro Eastern Maine League... and he named them the Green Moths as well. The Trenton Green Moths were,

in fact, a powerhouse in a league that stretched as far as Bradley, Milo, Corinna, Brewer, and Millinocket. Bill didn't have to go far to enjoy a game, either: the Green Moths' home field was conveniently located right behind his store and luncheonette.

Circa 1940 Schlotzhauer sold his business to a man named Edward Sutton. Sutton maintained the Green Moth name and the tradition of a combination grocery store and place to eat. He, however, did away with the baseball field. Around 1945 he constructed a cabin court where once stood an outfield and an infield.

Since 1985 the Green Moth has been owned and operated by Jeannie and John Merchant.

Photo, November 1994. Jeannie Merchant outside her restaurant. She's proud that everything she serves is made from scratch; and especially proud of the day that Billy Joel stopped in and bought one of her cookies. That was circa 1986 and Jeannie was still working part-time at a bank in Bar Harbor. But one of her staff telephoned her with the news and Jeannie still recalls that she screamed through the lobby of the bank : "Billy Joel just bought one of my cookies!"

58

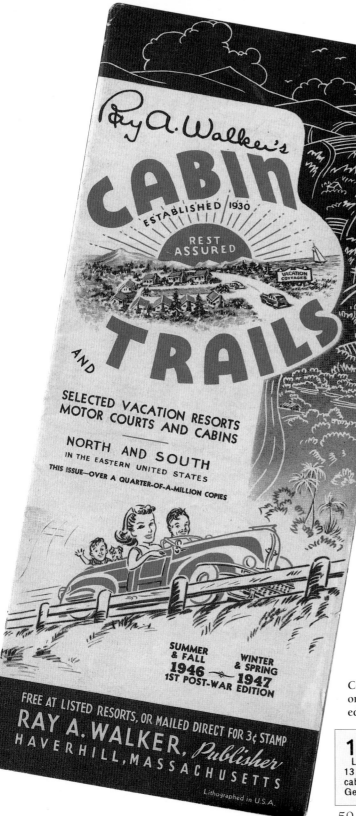

Jeannie, who's 41 and a native of Lee, Maine, grew up amid her parents' sporting camps in an atmosphere of lots of cooking and self-reliance. John, 42, is a native of Mt. Desert Island. He, too, liked the idea of being his own boss. So when the Green Moth came on the market the Merchants stepped up and bought it. When I asked Jeannie whether it was love at first sight, she laughed. It wasn't. The place had been allowed to go somewhat to pot. "But," she continued, "we could see its future potential due to its history and location." Nor have Jeannie and John been disappointed. They've completely done over the cabins, and converted the main building (the one pictured here) to a restaurant. Even the name has been altered: it's now the Green Moth Pancake and Chowder House, with "Green Moth" in smaller letters. That's because, Jeannie explains, "We're trying to get across what we sell and 'Green Moth' doesn't tell 'em anything." Have no fear, though, the Green Moth name is here to stay. Jeannie fully realizes the name's historical significance, adding "It's a landmark in the eyes of the local people."

Cover, *Cabin Trails* brochure, 1946-1947. The Green Moth was one of 30 Maine cabin courts listed in Ray Walker's first postwar edition of *Cabin Trails*. Below is what Ray had to say.

103 LST	The GREEN MOTH Rt. 3, 6 mi. S. of Ellsworth
	13 mi. from Bar Harbor, overlooking Cadillac Mt. New, large cabins, private showers. Restaurant, home-cooked food. General store. E.K.Sutton, prop. RFD 1, Ellsworth. Tel. 155W3.

Hager's
Waterville

"It was the classic ice cream parlor." That's how longtime *Waterville Morning Sentinel* columnist and unofficial city historian Clayton LaVerdiere recalls Hager's. Metal chairs with heart-shaped backs. Large glass mirrors. A soda fountain with a marble-topped counter. Hager's had it all. But mostly, further recalls Clayton, Hager's had the "irreplaceable aroma of sweets and ice cream concoctions that made it a very unique place on the main street."

Hager's had a long run on Main Street. It began as a fruit and confectionery shop in 1898. Proprietor was William A. Hager. Ice cream - homemade, of course - was added circa 1913. Of equal importance was the addition of Carl Cornforth. After a number of years of clerking at the shop, Cornforth became a partner, also circa 1913, and it was he who would carry Hager's to its greatest heights.

It's difficult now to imagine what a place like Hager's meant to Waterville in the years between the two World Wars. "It was a place we'd walk to - my sisters and I - on a Sunday afternoon," recollects 77-year old Rita Huard. "That's what we'd do for pleasure. We'd get a banana split or a hot fudge sundae and then we'd go walking all around. That was exciting." As Clayton ampli-

fies so well: "On Sunday afternoon people would get spiffed up and go out walking. Times were slower. Life was at a slow but delicious pace." And, in Waterville, people would say "Let's go to Hager's."

William A. Hager retired right around 1930, with Carl Cornforth becoming sole proprietor, the man responsible for most of Rita and Clayton's warm memories. But changing times eventually caught up with Hager's. It closed in 1954. Its site, on the first floor of the quite handsome 1887 three-story brick Boutelle Building at 113 Main Street, was occupied by Larry's Pharmacy for close to a decade, and was then vacant. In 1970 it became home to Village Barbers. Since 1982 it's been Headquarters Hairstyling.

Haines Theatre
Waterville

When it opened on February 7, 1918 the Haines Theatre was touted as "Maine's Handsomest Playhouse." Modeled after Boston's Majestic Theatre, it seated 1,300, about evenly divided between the orchestra and balcony. The decor featured a tasteful blend of gray, ivory, and gold, accentuated by the use of nearly 2,000 light bulbs. On the bill was a double movie feature, a vaudeville program of dancers, "clever singers," comedians, and a musical recital. Rounding it all out was a Hearst News Pictorial.

The opening generated great excitement. Almost too much excitement. The *Waterville Morning Sentinel* reported the next day that "A crowd collected shortly after 6 o'clock that nearly blocked the street. There was such a rush for seats that the show was delayed in starting and it was nearly midnight before the last of the spectators left."

The Haines maintained that sense of excitement for all its years. People I spoke with in Waterville universally remembered it with fervor. "We used to go every Saturday. We'd sit in the balcony - first row - and we'd meet all our classmates there," reminisced Rita Huard, now 77. "It was a nice theatre. It was a family theatre," are the words chosen by 73-year old Irene Roy. Clayton LaVerdiere, also 73, recalls that "The ushers all had natty uniforms. There was a feeling of class to the place." And it didn't really matter much what

was playing: "Any movie we saw was a conversation piece for the rest of the week." Clayton also recollects the time Haines' management held a "guess how many lightbulbs there are in the marquee" contest. "It was funny to walk by the theatre and see all these people looking up," he chuckles.

The Haines opened in February. It closed in February. Shortly after midnight on February 11, 1967, the theatre was rocked by what the *Morning Sentinel* described as an "explosion punctuated blaze." It took 85 firefighters to battle the conflagration, which shot flames 100 feet into the air. When it was over, there was nothing left that was worth saving. On the site, 175 Main Street, there is today a vest-pocket park.

Hat's Drive-In
Houlton

Talk about a pioneer! When Elvin Hatfield opened his Hat's Drive-In in 1952 he was the first person to offer pizza north of Bangor. "People didn't know what it looked like or how to eat it," laughs Elvin, now 76 and living in South Portland. Hat's was one of the few places north of Bangor to feature carhops. But they didn't go over as well as pizza, and Elvin "gave up on that" after a few seasons.

Elvin opened up a second restaurant in Houlton circa 1955. Watching over both eventually became a major headache. The biggest problem was that employees tended to give - rather then to sell - hot dogs and hamburgers to friends. "You couldn't be in two places at once," Elvin learned. He closed the drive-in in 1960. The building was subsequently razed. Its location on Military Street is now occupied by a small apartment building.

Courtesy of Maine Historic Preservation Commission, Augusta.

HAINES THEATRE, WATERVILLE, ME.

Postcard view, circa 1920. The Haines Theatre was named in honor of William T. Haines (1854-1919), a successful Waterville Lawyer and businessman who served Maine as governor from 1913 to 1915.

Hay's Drug Store on Congress Square as it glistened in a photo taken June 18, 1944. The structure was originally constructed, in 1826, as two stories. The third story was designed by Maine's best-known architect, John Calvin Stevens, in 1922. The building is today listed on the National Register of Historic Places.

Hay's Drug Store

Portland

Hay's Drug store was founded by 20-year old Henry Homer Hay in 1841. Born in Waterford, Maine in 1820, he was the youngest of 12 children. His father, grandfather and great-grandfather had all been physicians, but Henry Homer decided that the drug business was more to his liking.

The original H.H. Hay Drug Store was located on Fore Street, just above Exchange, but as business grew Hay moved his operation, circa 1843, to Market (now Monument) Square. By 1856 he'd outgrown that location, too. The result was a move down Middle Street to where Middle and Free Streets meet. Here he was almost wiped out when the Great Fire swept through Portland in 1866, being spared only because a 40-man bucket brigade kept the flames at bay.

Henry Homer Hay passed away in 1895 but the business that he'd launched was successfully carried on by his sons Charles and Edward (and later his grandson Merrill). The firm was incorporated as H.H. Hay and Son in 1905, and the store at Middle and Free was remodeled and enlarged that same year.

It was in 1912, however, that H.H. Hay and Son took its boldest step: it opened a second store, at the junction of Congress and Free Streets on Congress Square. Here, in a resplendent flatiron-ish looking building designed by noted Portland architect Charles C. Clapp in 1826, H.H. Hay and Son went on to its greatest fame. And much of that fame centered around the store's quite marvelous first-floor soda fountain and second-floor Dutch Den Soda Shop. The Dutch Den featured posters of Holland and tulip-filled window boxes. The fountain was famous for its own super rich ice cream. Both floors featured homemade muffins, cupcakes, and pies, and a specially ground coffee that came from New York.

The fountain and the Dutch Den each flourished during the Depression when H.H. Hay served a businessman's lunch for 35¢ and a steak for $1.00. Hay's pea soup, the Saturday special, was supposedly so irresistable that Rudy Vallee's father, Charles, came in from Westbrook to partake of it most every week.

After World War II the Dutch Den lost its popularity and was closed. Overall, H.H. Hay and Son began to experience financial difficulties in the 1950s. The firm was placed in receivership in September, 1963, and sold by the Hay family in November, 1964. The storied soda fountain served its last taste treats on June 30, 1972. Its closing was front page stuff in the next day's *Evening Express*.

The pharmaceutical side of H.H. Hay and Son limped along until 1979. In October of that year, it, too, closed. The building, as magnificent as ever, is today occupied by Douglas Harding Rare Books. I recently asked employee Kevin Harding if people still come in to reminisce about the soda fountain's glory days. He smiled and replied, "They sure do."

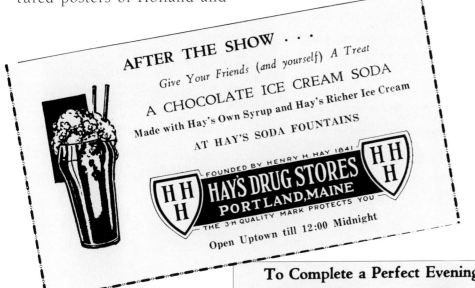

A pair of ads from the days when Hay's soda fountain was humming, 1940.

Helen's
Machias

What is today a Down East restaurant landmark began as an ice cream stand in downtown Machias in 1950: "A little hole in the wall," as present-day co-proprietor Gary Hanscom phrases it. It was the brainchild of then 42-year old Larry Mugnai and his wife Helen. And their ice cream was fine, but a number of patrons suggested it would be nice to be able to get a sandwich and a cup of coffee as well, and Larry and Helen obliged. They expanded in late 1950/early 1951, and again in the mid-fifties. The construction of nearby Cutler Towers by the Navy in 1957 really spurred growth: suddenly there were people from all over the country enjoying what the Mugnais were cooking up.

In 1976, after over a quarter of a century on the job day in and day out, Larry and Helen sold their creation to Bob and Joan Carter. It is Bob who is responsible for today's Helen's: he noticed the former Machias Box Company/H. Blaine Davis Home Supply building site vacant just east of town... and decided it should be the once and future Helen's. The Carters opened the new Helen's in 1983. For two years they kept the original location open, too, finally consolidating operations in the newer and much larger Helen's in late 1985.

Present-day proprietors Judy and Gary Hanscom took over in 1988. Gary, who's 47 and a native of Machias, and who was making good money driving a trailor truck, admits that buying Helen's was "scary." But he's delighted he took the risk. "It's the best move I ever made in my lifetime," he says, quickly adding: "other than marrying my wife, of course."

Photo, August 1994. Originally located at 34 Main Street in the heart of Machias, Helen's moved to this location on lower Main Street/U.S. Route 1 in 1983. Have Gary and Judy ever thought of changing the restaurant's name... to, say, something like "Judy's?" "Nope," answers Judy: "We're too well known. People hunt for us."

Photo, August 1994. Gary and Judy's daughter-in-law Terri Barker serves up a slice of the strawberry pie that's made Helen's famous statewide and then some. What explains the pie's popularity? Well, Larry Mugnai and his sister Esther get credit for the original recipe. Gary and Judy get credit for continuing to serve healthy-sized portions. Plus, kids Gary, "There are no calories in there: we take 'em all out."

64

Nineteen year-old Angela Makosiej of Gardiner was the carhop of the day the day I stopped by the Hi-Hat. Here she is serving up a cheese-burger tray. Angela describes carhopping as "fun." What she enjoys the most about it is the chance to get outside. "It's not so much fun in the rain, though," she does admit.

Photos, July 1994. Thirty-three year old Kirk Cahill, who shares the role of head chef with his brother, Todd, 28, is proud that the Hi-Hat still uses Ernie's origi-nal recipes for both onion rings and clams-in-batter. He's also proud of the daily spe-cials and that everything is homemade. Things like real mashed potatoes do make a difference, he told me. I didn't disagree.

Hi-Hat Drive-In
Farmingdale

Old drive-in restaurants never die. Not in Farmingdale, any-way. What's now the Hi-Hat is in its 51st season... and while the drive-in side of the business isn't going so strong anymore, at least it's still going. And for that we can be thankful.

What is today the Hi-Hat began as Ernie's Lunch in 1944. In 1955-1956, proprietor Ernie Thulen (1923-1977) changed the name of his restaurant to Ernie's Drive-In. Why not: it was, after all, the "fabulous fifties," and the automobile was the center of the universe. One

person who recalls those glory days well is 66-year old Paul Gregoire of Augusta, who ate at Ernie's with his wife Norma just about every week in the late 1950s and early 1960s. He still smacks his lips over the drive-in's chicken-in-the-basket. "In fact, anything they had in a bas-ket was good," he sums up. In 1974, Ernie's was purchased by Ted and Vi Cahill. Both Ted and Vi were originally from Aroost-ook County; both had moved to Connecticut, where they met; both were anxious to move back to Maine and raise a family. "They saved their pennies," as their son Kirk puts it, and moved back in 1967. After first

buying a restaurant in Augusta, the couple bought Ernie's, changed its name to the Hi-Hat, and both switched to an open-all-year operation and doubled the size of the din-ing room in 1981. In the late 1980s they eliminated evening and night-time service. "It was just too hard to get good help," Kirk explained. Hours are now 6:00 AM to 3:00 PM.

Mostly, though, the Cahills have concentrated on indoor dining. The result is that the carhop business, which was the Hi-Hat's "bread and butter" all through the 1970s, now accounts for less than 5% of receipts. But the Hi-Hat *is* still a real drive-in. And, Kirk assures me, it will continue to be. So drive on in to 232 Maine Street/Route 201, turn on your headlights ("Lights On For Service"), and enjoy.

Photo, circa 1946. This was Hyacinth Hodgman's first permanent roadside edifice. Constructed in 1946, it replaced a tiny 10' x 8' cabin-like structure (that now stands, incidentally, about 200 yards down the road toward Gray and is part of the Echo O' the Morn Farm's roadside stand). The apple tree pictured on the left still stands, too, although it's somewhat weathered by its years. Joyce has placed a sign on it that reads: Please Keep Off: This Tree Is Very Old.

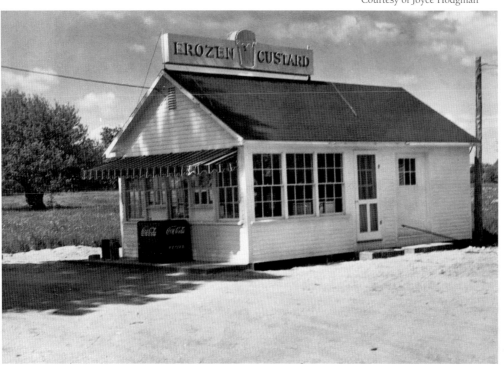

Courtesy of Joyce Hodgman

Hodgman's Frozen Custard
New Gloucester

The *Encyclopedia America* defines frozen custard as "similar to ice cream in composition except that it must contain not less than 1.4% by weight of egg yolk solids for plain flavors (such as vanilla) and 1.28% for bulky flavors (such as strawberry)." Try telling that to people who line up at Hodgman's on Lewiston Road in New Gloucester, however, and all you're likely to get in response is a "Huh?" They're there for the taste, not the chemical analysis.

That New Gloucester is king of the Maine frozen custard world is quite by accident. In 1945 a woman from Wisconsin signed up to be a custard vendor at the New Gloucester Fairgrounds. She dutifully arrived... only to find out that the fairgrounds' season had been cancelled. Disgusted, she decided to pack it in with respect to frozen custard, and advertised her custard machine for sale. The buyer was Hyacinth Hodgman, then owner/operator of a chicken farm on the same basic site as today's Hodgman's. What possessed Hyacinth to buy the machine? "It fascinated her, I guess," ventures daughter-in-law and present proprietor Joyce Hodgman, "just the idea of having something like that in town." Plus Hyacinth was already selling eggs roadside and so had somewhat of a built-in customer base with which to begin.

Joyce describes her mother-in-law's initial frozen custard stand as "ramshackle." And small. There were no set hours. Business was good, though, and for summer season number two, 1946, Hyacinth had a new and much larger building constructed. Almost half a century later that building - with three additions to it - is still going strong. And so are frozen custard sales. Joyce credits much of her success to the fact that she still uses the original machine and

66

Photo, August 1994. In addition to the original machine and the original formula, there's been one other constant at Hodgman's: its wonderful rooftop neon sign. "I'm real proud of that sign," says Joyce. She deserves to be. It's a dandy!

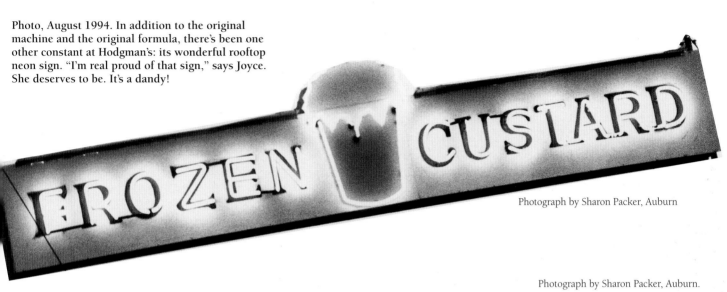

the original formula. Plus, she's quick to add, "I've been blessed with wonderful help."

Much of that help has come from local high school-age kids. Then there's the family, too: husband Kenneth, daughters Donna and Kathy, son Scott all pitch in to create what is truly a family business. Family and frozen custard: who could ask for anything more?

Photo, August 1994. Hodgman's is open from Mother's Day through Labor Day. Here's how it looks most any nice evening.

Grand Opening SATURDAY NIGHT

7:00 O'clock — October 30

"LISBON BOWLING CENTER"

Lisbon Street   —Lisbon Falls—   Maine

One of the Newest and Most Modern Bowling Recreation Centers in the New England States.

- **AUTOMATIC PIN SPOTTERS**

No Pin Boys!

- **CIRCULAR UPHOLSTERED SEATS**

for the bowlers.

Comfortable Seats for the Spectators.

- **FOUNTAIN SERVICE AND LIGHT LUNCHES**

We take pride in opening the New "Bowling Center" to the sportsfans in this area of the state, and we respectfully ask your support in helping keep this a clean establishment of entertainment!

Remember the name "LISBON BOWLING CENTER." Alley appointments will be accepted. Open every afternoon and evening!

Proprietors: **E. L. Robinson & Son**   Manager: **Melvin Robinson**

Hogan's Good Time Lanes
Lisbon Falls

What was founded by E.L. Robinson in 1948 as the Lisbon Bowling Center became Hogan's Good Time Lanes in 1981. And for Frank and Pam Hogan the lanes have lived up to the name: they've had good times there. "Working with kids, that's the most fun," says Frank. Both Frank and Pam agree that the seniors are fun, too, and smile as they recall the circa 1989 night when one of the over-80 regulars turned in a masterful 160-plus game.

But even good times can get tiring. In 1993, Frank, then 34, and Pam, 32, decided it was time to move on to new adventures, and ended up selling to local businessmen Mike Goslin and Wayne Parent in August 1994. Good luck to Mike and Wayne, and to Pam and Frank... and to the Good Time Lanes.

Frank and Pam pose for a final photo as proprietors of Hogan's Good Time Lanes, August, 1994

Postcard view, circa 1915. Take a stroll down this same street - Beach Street - today and you'll find that not all that much has really changed.

Courtesy of Maine Historic Preservation Commission, Augusta.

Holland Theatre and Bowling Alley

York Beach

Call it luck or call it a minor miracle: both the theatre and the bowling alley that brothers Dan and John Holland opened in "downtown" York Beach in 1913 are still hale and hardy and in operation today... over eight decades later.

The theatre, called the Holland into the 1920s, was built to be a showplace. A 1923 ad proclaimed that it gave York Beach "That

'BIG CITY' Touch." The bowling alley, too, gave a nice touch. Located directly across Beach Street from the theatre, it consisted of ten lanes at first; enlarged to 12 after the first season. What's worthy of note is that originally the alley opened onto Beach Street. Now it opens onto Short Sands Beach. The switch was made in 1951.

Today both the theatre - now the York Beach Cinema - and the lanes - the York Beach Bowling Alleys - appear to be in good

hands. Since 1978 the owner of the theatre has been Portland native Peter Clayton. He's proud of the theatre's original tin walls, 1930s' Peerless projectors, and that it attracts "a lot of kids and families." The bowling alley has been owned by the Bill Burnham family, from Dover, New Hampshire, since 1987. Bill, Jr. manages the lanes. Ask him to show you the original Brunswick Bauke-Collender embossed brass plaques that adorn each ball return rack. They really are pretty special.

69

Hotel Rockland
Rockland

What became the Hotel Rockland was constructed as the Lynde Hotel by local livery stable and stagecoach magnate George Lynde in 1870. By 1882 the hotel had changed hands... and its name. It became the St. Nicholas Hotel, with David Bird and Joseph Nutter the proprietors. From 1882 to circa 1915 the hotel changed hands several more times, but retained St. Nicholas as its name. A 1906 ad claimed it possessed the "Nicest Rooms In The City."

Circa 1915 the hotel was purchased by M. Frank Donahue, who gave it the name "Rockland." It was a name that would remain - more or less - until the hotel's demise. It's necessary to state "more or less" because the hotel was named the "New Hotel Rockland" for a decade or so in the 1930s and 1940s.

By the 1950s the hotel's name was back to just "Hotel Rockland" again. The problem was that the 1950s didn't last very long as far as the venerable hostelry was concerned. Rockland has suffered three great fires. The first was in 1853; the second in 1920. The third erupted the evening of Friday, December 12, 1952. Members of both the Rockland Chamber of Commerce and the Order of the Eastern Star had just begun their respective dinners at the Rockland. Neither group ever got to finish.

Before the blaze was contained - with help from a heavy rain and a dozen fire departments from as far away as Augusta, Bath, Brunswick, and Bangor - 22 buildings were demolished. The Hotel Rockland - by then part of the Acheson Hotels' chain - was one of them.

Today the hotel's former site, at the southeast corner of Main and Park Streets, is occupied by a deserted Sears' store. But tap most any oldtimer on the shoulder, ask about the Rockland... and you'll find it's still quite fresh in their memory. "It was a big beautiful building with a porch on the front," recalls 80-year old Evelyn Merrifield. "It had rugs all the way up the stairs," is what 75-year old Hank Judecki remembers first and foremost. "The people who ran it made everyone feel at home," recollects Betty Madore, 72, while her friend, 79-year old Mildred Brannan, chimes in with "Good home cooking in a nice atmosphere." "It was *the* place to go for banquets and gatherings," she's quick to add. How did Mildred feel when the Rockland burned down? "I felt we'd lost a milestone," she replies slowly. "An era was gone."

New Hotel Rockland, Rockland, Maine

Postcard view, circa 1945. In 1947, the cast and crew of the Twentieth Century-Fox movie *Deep Waters* - filmed on Vinalhaven - stayed at the Hotel Rockland. Stars included Dana Andrews, Ed Begley, Jean Peters, Cesar Romero, and Dean Stockwell. It was a big deal. "Everbody was all excited," vividly recalls Freddie Goodnow. Freddie, who was ten at the time, also vividly recalls that he got a bunch of autographs. Some things you never forget.

Photo, September 1994. This giant milk carton serves as a beacon for Houlton Farms' Presque Isle dairy bar. Presque Isle was the company's inaugural dairy bar... and it has traditionally been tops in sales among the three outlets. Its location on Route 1 doesn't hurt.

Photo, September 1994. Here's Beth Riley, 16, of Houlton on the job at Houlton. And what does Beth like the best about the job? "I get to eat ice cream," she replies without so much as a trace of hesitation. Good answer, Beth.

Houlton Farms Dairy Bars
Caribou, Houlton, Presque Isle

In its 45th year of operation, 1983, the folks at Houlton Farms came up with the idea of a dairy bar. Door-to-door milk sales were down and the company was sitting with an underutilized delivery truck depot on Route 1 in Presque Isle. Why not convert it to a dairy bar? Why not, indeed! The idea worked so well that Houlton farms added a second dairy bar, in Caribou in 1987, and a third, in Houlton, in 1988. Now, a dozen years after it all began, dairy bar sales account for a substantial share of the dairy's total business. Of perhaps equal importance, chuckles co-proprietor Alice Lincoln, is that "It's a fun part of the business." What makes it fun, not surprisingly, is the creation of new dishes. "We're always coming up with something new," Alice says unequivocally. Some of these new concoctions flop, of course. Others become big sellers. When I visited in the summer of 1994 the best seller, far and away, was the Brownie A La Mode. Also hot were Old Fashioned Ice Cream Sodas, Homemade Waffle Sundaes, Rainbow Supremes, and Awful Awfuls (which, just in case you didn't know, is a thick frappe with ice cream on top).

Houlton Farms was founded in 1938 by Alan H. Clark, a Houlton native who thought the time was ripe for a centralized dairy operation in his home town. In 1977 he sold to Milton B. Lambert, Jr., who in turn sold, in 1981, to Alice, her husband Leonard, and their sons Eric and Jim. It was Alice and Leonard who thought the dairy bar was a good idea. How right they were!

71

Howe's Confectionery Store
Rumford

"The man who brought fudge to Rumford." "Pioneer movie man of Oxford County." "The popcorn man." Take your pick. All apply to Charles Eli Howe.

Born in Hanover, Maine in 1871, C.E. Howe set himself up in the retail trade in Rumford in 1896. His was sort of a combined candy and fruit and stationery and toy store, plus a soda fountain, too. A special business supplement to the *Rumford Falls Times* of December 15, 1900 described C.E.'s establishment as "inviting" and "up to date," further proclaiming that his shop "will be Santa Claus' headquarters for confectionery, toys, nuts, fruits, etc."

Well, Santa was to be in for a very special treat that Christmas. The treat was fudge! Invented in the late 1880s, fudge slowly captured the hearts and taste buds of America in the 1890s. Charles E. Howe appears to have been the person who introduced it to Rumfordites. That alone, of course, should have assured his place in Rumford immortality. But C.E. was not a man to rest on his laurels. He went on to become a pioneer movie mogul around town: as early as 1912 he'd rent a hall and put on a picture show. In later years, he was almost universally known as "the popcorn man." Rumford historian Stuart Martin recalls that C.E. "had a popcorn machine and he'd bring it to fairs and other public functions." "He was a character," remembers former neighbor Patty Martineau, but quickly adds that he was a real good-natured guy, too. "He always made lots of popcorn for Halloween and we'd always hit his house first... because we always knew we'd get fresh popcorn."

The man who introduced fudge to Rumford died in the early 1960s. His former store, located beneath the Rumford Hotel at 70 Congress Street, is no more. The hotel, along with its various retail outlets, was demolished by fire in November of 1929. F.W. Woolworth later constructed a 5¢ and 10¢ store on the site. Today even that is history: the former Woolworth is occupied by Duffy's Discount Store.

Ad, March 1900. The century was new. And so was fudge.

Jack's Lunch
Bath

John J. Conroy - the "Jack" of Jack's Lunch - was virtually born to be in the diner business. His dad, John E., was operating a lunch cart in Lynn, Massachusetts when Jack came into the world in 1890. The Conroys moved to John E.'s home town of Bangor some time after the turn of the century. There, too, the elder Conroy operated a lunch cart, at 24 1/2 Harlow Street. In 1917 the family moved to Bath, where father and son operated the Star Cafe at 22-24 Front Street. After a few years in Sanford, John J. returned to Bath where, circa 1923, he opened his own place - Jack's Lunch, of course - at 89-91 Centre Street.

Actually, Jack's lunch car sported two names: Jack's and Ramble Inn. But his son, longtime Bath resident Donald Conroy, recalls people used just the Jack's name. Donald also recalls the diner as being small (10 stools/no tables), being open from 4:00 PM to 1:00 or 2:00 AM, and being noted for its sandwiches and its pies. Especially the pies: Jack's wife, Annie, and mother, Lettie, did the baking... and are remembered as being mighty good at it. Their cream pies were especially favored!

Along about 1934, however, another love came into Jack's life. It seems that a diner employee, one Red Hart, had a

Jack's Lunch was most likely a "Worcester," manufactured by the Worcester Lunch Car Company, of Worcester, Massachusetts. The ornate windows are especially worthy of note: known as "flash glass," they very often - as with Jack's - featured goddesses.

Actually, Jack Conroy was a minor diner magnate: he also owned two other companion lunch cars he set up during the summer season. Favorite locales included Old Orchard Beach, Sanford, the East Deering section of Portland (on Veranda Street, just off Washington Avenue), and Boothbay Harbor.

In fact, the Boothbay Harbor model yet survives...sort of. It sits, slowly deteriorating, above the Boothbay Railway Village. (The Village would *love* to find someone who'd like to take it home and restore it.) Jack Conroy, himself, passed away at age 72 in East Hampden, Maine in 1962.

Photo, circa 1925.   Courtesy of Maine Historic Preservation Commission, Augusta.

habit of bumming cigarettes from Jack. Jack countered by installing a cigarette vending machine. Then in its infancy, the new-fangled machine proved a hit. Other businesspeople wanted to know where they could get one. Jack obliged by setting up his own vending territory, stretching from Bath to Bangor. He sold the diner, circa 1935, to focus on his machines.

After Jack's departure the diner passed through several other proprietors - Russell Phinney; Eunice and Howard Poolos (who dubbed it the Silver Diner); and William Ouellette (also spelled "Willette") - before being demolished in the very early 1950s. Its former site, just east of the railroad tracks, is now occupied by a part of the parking lot for Steego Auto Parts.

Jay Hill Drive-In Theatre
Jay

The tale of the Jay Hill Drive-In could well be called the tale of two drive-ins. Opened in July of 1953, the mere mention of the theatre brings a heady smile to the face of all who frequented it as a patron. "It was fun; everybody used to go there," beams 33-year old Gene Barker of Jay, who remembers the drive-in both as a teenager and as a toddler who enjoyed the theatre's playground. Craig Viotto, now of North Jay, recalls going to the Jay Hill with his grandparents: "It was like a family thing." For 40-year old Patty Donald of North Jay the drive-in meant romance: "It was always neat to go there with your boyfriend." And 41-year old Carol Ross of Wilton sums up many of the other reasons people like drive-ins: "It didn't cost a lot and you could bring your own snacks; you had the big screen; you could talk back and forth among yourselves

Cover of coming attractions' flyer, 1956

without anybody else getting upset." Another summation came from 52-year old Bill Lee who used to drive from Weld to go to the Jay Hill: "It was something to do."

But talk to 60-year old Isabelle "Casey" Hodgkins or her daughter, Kathy Young-Groder, and one gets a very different perspective on life at the drive-in. Casey and

her late husband, Charlie Young, bought into the theatre circa 1964. By 1970 they owned all of it...and "terrible" is how Casey characterizes the experience. "You had to be there every night all summer long", says she, adding that it was "just hard work."

Daughter Kathy seconds her mother's view, calling the drive-in years "a nightmare." She does laugh, though, when she recalls her father's green paint trick. It seems that kids would often sneak into the theatre via a hole under the fence. Charlie would often paint the botton of the fence green just before showtime, so he could tell who'd snuck in. Did he then oust them from the theatre? "No, he just chuckled," smiles Kathy. "He felt the joke was on them."

Another happening that brings smiles - more or less - to Casey's and Kathy's face is the locally-infamous Ordinance #26. In the early 1970s Charlie started to run X-rated films at the drive-in. It was a way to combat television. But it didn't set well with some key townspeople. The result was an ordinance, passed in March of 1972, that prohibited "the operation of an outdoor motion picture theatre unless said theatre is suitably screened to prevent the projected picture or projection light from being visable from any public way or public place." To remain in operation Charlie and Casey had to erect a 45-foot high wall along Route 4.

Casey recounts, however, that it was vandalism that finally caused the closing of the theatre in 1974-1975. The former theatre's site, on Route 4 just down and across from Bill Lee's Imagination Leather Craft Shop, is today an open field.

Kennebec Fruit Company
Lisbon Falls

Ask Frank Anicetti, Jr. about Moxie and chances are you'll get a veritable college lecture course. Moxie 101. But that's as it should be. Frank *is*, after all, Mr. Moxie!

It all began in 1978 when Frank

was photographed behind the wheel of an antique Moxie promotional vehicle in a local parade. The photo was syndicated coast to coast, and almost before he knew it Frank found himself aiding in the research for a book entitled *The Moxie Mystique*. When the book came out in 1982, Frank hosted what he thought would be an intimate book signing at his Kennebec Fruit store. It, instead, turned out to be "a real blast," with over 500 people in attendance. Next thing, folks from all over were bringing in Moxie memorabilia...which Frank dutifully displayed in the store. Now, 13 years later, Kennebec Fruit is a one-stop Moxie museum and souvenir shop. Moxie shirts, hats, posters, decals. Frank has them all. Plus Moxie. And, best of all, Moxie Ice Cream. Frank has long made his own ice cream but what is now his best-

selling flavor came into being because a Moxie salesman bet a case of soda that Frank couldn't make Moxie Ice Cream. The salesman lost the bet!

P.S. Moxie, a soft drink once so popular that its name became a part of our language - to have "moxie" is to have spunk - was a true Yankee invention. The inventor was Dr. Augustine Thompson. The year was 1876. The town was Union. The state was Maine.

The Kennebec Fruit Company and Frank, 54, serving up a Moxie Ice Cream cone. Both photos, August 1994. Kennebec Fruit was founded in Bath circa 1908. Frank's store, begun by his grandfather Lumberto in 1914, is today the last of 14 Kennebec Fruits that once dotted Maine. Stop in at 2 Main Street/Route 196 and admire the original tin ceiling, marble counter, and cherry "back bar." Be sure to enjoy a Moxie Ice Cream cone, too. Better yet, visit on Moxie Day - an annual bash the second Saturday in July - and you can watch a good 20,000 other people enjoy one as well.

Postcard view, circa 1935. A very definite highlight in the Lancey House's long and illustrious history came in June 1955. Dwight D. Eisenhower, the president of the United States, was passing through Pittsfield on his way from Skowhegan to Bangor. Impressed by the warmth of Pittsfield's welcome, Ike stopped the motorcade, alighted from his car, and made an impromptu speech to the thousands gathered on Main Street. His speech, naturally enough, was made smack dab in front of - you guessed it! - the Lancey House.

Lancey House Hotel, Pittsfield, Maine

Ad, circa 1950. Joseph R. Cianchette, founder of the Cianbro Corp., owned the Lancey House from 1945 to 1960.

Lancey House
Pittsfield

If you've ever wondered where Easy Street is...well, it's in Pittsfield. And it was the site of the original Lancey House. Opened in 1830, this Lancey House served the community until 1864 when Isaac Lancey - known locally as "The Prince of Hosts" - moved operations a short distance to the corner of Main Street and Hunnewell Avenue. There he constructed an inn that photos of the day show to be four stories in height and impressive in looks. This second edition operated until badly damaged by fire in October 1906. It took five years, but the Lancey House was finally repaired and refurbished and opened for business - as a three-story structure - in 1911. This third and last Lancey House - the one that's pictured here - provided food and shelter until it,

too, was badly damaged by fire, again in October, in 1965. Only this time the Lancey House was not repaired and refurbished. It was torn down..

In its 120 years what distinguished the Lancey House - all three of them - was its warmth, well-kept rooms, and friendly, courteous service. And its food! Goose, duck, stuffed shad, salmon, leg of mutton, venison: such were the staples of the Lancey's table. Traveling salesmen reputedly loved to be snowbound at the Lancey, able to eat to their heart's content. And a 1985 *Bangor Daily News'* article recalled that "Bangor's well-heeled were chauffeured down to the inn to dine on duck."

On the noted hostelry's site, 60 Main Street, there is today a Peoples Heritage office. Duck is not served.

Lano's Diner
South Portland

Although he was only eight at the time, Jimmy Lano still remembers the party that was thrown for his family and himself just before they left Albania for America in 1921. "When you come to America you're going to find gold on the streets": that's what they said at the party.

Well, Jimmy didn't find any streets of gold. But he did find a land of opportunity... if you were willing to work for it. And he was. In the span from 1921 to 1939 Jimmy worked at 22 different jobs in and around Portland, and still found time to graduate from Portland High School in 1933... always with one goal in mind. "Every move I made I made a dollar more," he says proudly, "until I had enough money to buy my own place."

That place of his own transpired in two steps. The first occurred

Courtesy of Jimmy Lano, South Portland

Lano's Diner as it appeared in a circa 1946 photograph. The diner was most likely "homemade"; i.e., not constructed by a diner manufacturing company. It seated 28 people and employed five, including Jimmy who did the cooking.

in 1937 when a Nissen route-man, George Chute, suggested to Jimmy that Route 1 in the Cash Corner section of South Portland would be the perfect place for an eatery. "Jimmy," he said, "put a lunch car there and you'll make a barrel of money." Jimmy, then working in a sandwich shop on High Street, agreed... but was in no financial position to do anything about it.

Stage two came about by accident. A full two years later, in 1939, Jimmy happened to be riding through Cash Corner and there, voila, sat a small diner right on *his* dream plot. But all was not lost: Jimmy did a little investigating and found that the diner's owner, Gus Shaw, was not very happy. He had paid to have the diner moved from Kittery, was commuting from Windham every day, and was not taking in enough money to make it worthwhile. Jimmy made an offer of $500. Gus said "No." Jimmy made an offer of $1000. Gus said "Yes."

Jimmy named his diner Jimmy's Diner and operated it until 1941, when he leased it out in order to concentrate his efforts on a diner (George's Diner, which Jimmy renamed the Tip Top Diner) on Water Street in Bath. Then came four years in the military, courtesy of the U.S. Army. His South Portland diner, meanwhile, continued on as Ginger and Shirley's Diner until

1946 when Jimmy took over the reins once more. This time around, though, he named it Lano's Diner, and Lano's it would remain until 1949.

In 1948-1949 Jimmy fulfilled a fantasy one step above owning and operating his own diner: he built - and owned and operated - his own full-scale restaurant. Named Lano's Restaurant, it opened for business in June, 1949, at 300 Main Street, just across from the diner's location at 285 Main.

With the opening of the restaurant, Jimmy closed his diner. It sat vacant until 1951 when it was purchased by Alva Coron and moved down Route 1 to Scarborough. There, renamed the Raceway Diner, it was set up

just south of Scarborough Downs. A circa 1953 fire caused the diner to have to be rebuilt. A second fire, circa 1957, destroyed it completely. The site is today occupied by Tire Warehouse.

Jimmy Lano operated Lano's Restuarant (now the Mandarin House) until his retirement in 1972. He today resides in South Portland with Hope, his wife of 52 years. All these decades later, what is Jimmy proudest of with respect to his former diner? The truckers: "I had all these truckers from up north going to Boston. They'd all stop," he told me in a May, 1994 interview. "When you see trucks in a diner you know it's good food."

Courtesy of Jimmy Lano, South Portland

Here's another circa 1946 view of Lano's. On the site today, just to the right of Young's Auto Sales, there is what can be best described as a field of pavement.

Lewiston Drive-In Theatre
Lewiston

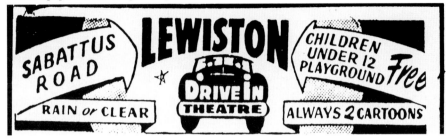

The Lewiston Drive-In Theatre opened to fanfare galore on July 1, 1949. It was, after all, the area's first drive-in. And it was big, with a 600-car capacity. And it was modern: the owners, Lockwood & Gordon Enterprises of Boston, spared no expense. The result was what the *Lewiston Evening Journal* touted as "one of the most modern outdoor theatres in the East." There were even, glory be, eight "traffic directors" to guide patrons to a suitable parking spot.

In between its opening and its closing 36 years later the Lewiston Drive-In was your typical drive-in. It was a "Passion Pit" for some; a place to bring the family for others. Fifty-two year old Claire Ward of Lewiston was in the latter category: she and her husband would bring their four kids to the "real corny, real square" shows. They'd make the night complete with soft drinks - which they'd bring from home - and popcorn - which they'd buy at the concession stand. "The popcorn was great," Claire vividly recalls even though her memories are from 1963 into the early 1970s. For Gordon Wilcox, 56, of North Monmouth, the drive-in was also a family thing. He'd go with his three children: "Being there with the kids was a little adventure; something out of the ordinary."

For 56-year old Bill Lawler of Auburn, however, the Lewiston Drive-In brings back 1950s' high school glory days. He'd either go with a bunch of Edward Little male buddies or on a double date. Either way, what Bill recalls most is his Nash Rambler with the seats that would fold down...and that two of the group would often hide in the trunk. Alas, though, Bill reports that eventually theatre management "got wise and started charging by the carload" rather than by the individual.

The "deepest" recollections of the drive-in came via a friend, Sharon Packer of Auburn. She remembers watching shows with her sons Jason and Andrew in the early 1980s. Sharon became downright excited as she shared what she terms "the mystery of the big screen and the dark car: there you are enclosed in your own little space. The car is familiar. And there's that big screen in front of you." It yields, she summed up, "an intimacy that you just don't get in a regular theatre."

By 1985, however, the Lewiston Drive-in was being eyed as more than just a place to watch movies. New Hampshire native Bob Foss thought the site perfect for a mobile home park and sales office. He purchased the site in July of that year, but allowed the drive-in to finish what would be its final season. The last features - *Gremlins*, and *Oh God! You Devil*, with George Burns - were shown on Labor Day, September 2. The theatre was then razed. On the site, 1149 Sabattus Street, there now stands Country Lane Estates and Country Lane Homes.

Lewiston Oyster and Chop House
Lewiston

I like this ad. And it certainly sends a message: you get a lot to eat so why not come on down and join us for a meal or two or three? Actually, though, little is known about the Oyster and Chop House's contribution to Lewiston/Auburn culinary delights. It appears to have been opened in 1913 by Louis and George Papan at what had long been an address of distinction for area restaurants: 134 Lisbon Street was previously home to both Fred W. Albee's Albee Cafe, and Shailer's, whose proprietor, William H. Shailer, also owned the locally well-known Exchange Hotel for a time.

The Papans operated their establishment for four years or so, until circa 1917. They then disappear from all subsequent city directories. Their restaurant's site was later home to, at one time or another, the P & Q Shop, Silverman's Ladies' Clothing, Sears, Roebuck, and Thom McAn shoes. On the site now is a relatively new structure. It houses a no-longer-in-operation Peoples Heritage office.

Clean and Polite Service   Tel. 177-M   Prices Modarate

I am hungry   So am I   I was   So was I   You won't be if you all eat at

LEWISTON OYSTER AND CHOP HOUSE 134 Lisbon St. Lewiston

Ad, September 1914. The Papans may have been shortlived in the operation of their restaurant but no one can fault them for lack of originality in their advertising.

Lincoln House
Lincoln

Augusta had its Augusta House. Caribou had its Vaughn House. Pittsfield had its Lancey House. And Lincoln had its Lincoln House. And it had it for a long, long time.

What became the Lincoln House was constructed as a private residence by local merchant William P. Leighton circa 1836. His "dream house," however, proved too costly for Leighton. Within a year he sold it to one James Merrill. Three changes of ownership later, in 1858, the structure became a hotel. It also became a gathering place. Accounts of the day indicate, for example, that the Lincoln House served as the town "news center" during the turbulent years of the Civil War: the news of the conflict arrived via the mail stage and many's the day a crowd would assemble to greet the stage and to share newspaper and dispatch accounts of Antietam, Bull Run, Gettysburg, and elsewhere. Ironically, perhaps the most noted guest in the hotel's long existence was Confederate General James Longstreet, who stopped at the Lincoln House for a cocktail after the war was over, in September of 1869.

The Great Dramatic Regulars, an acting company, was organized in Lincoln in 1875. Both their rehearsals and their performances were held in the Lincoln

House. A Mr. Metcalf was in charge. He was a stern taskmaster. One of the Regulars would later recall: "Mr. Metcalf was a stickler for the proprieties and used to stop the dancers if anyone got off the beat of the music. Once he stopped the dancers because one of them was chewing gum."

The Lincoln House was, of course, also an eating establishment. And a respected one, at that. An 1891 description stated that "The cuisine will be found very satisfactory, the table being supplied with an abundance of seasonable food at all times of the year and is neatly served."

Several additions were made to the Lincoln House in the last two decades of the 1800s, and by the turn of the century it stood an imposing four stories high. Alas, however, the grand old establishment was not to see the turn of another century. From 1915 until 1945 it was owned and operated by Fred J. Kelley, noted for "an excellent cuisine and a genial manner." In 1945 Kelley sold to Robert Burr, who continued operations until 1958. In that year - the year of the Lincoln House's 100th birthday as a hotel - it, in the words of a *Bangor Daily News* article, came "face to face with modern times." It was demolished in March 1958. On the site there now stands the Lincoln House All Brick Motel, an Irving Gas Station/Mainway Food Store, and a former Key Bank office building.

Lincoln Theatre
Damariscotta

In the dozen decades since it was constructed in 1875, the Lincoln Theatre has been host to just about everything under the Damariscotta sun. Roller skating, basketball, dog shows, talent contests, graduations, political orations, military drills, plus countless plays, vaudeville performances, and movies, movies, movies: they've all played "the Linc." The dressing room walls are testimony to it. They're lined with the names of almost 100 years of performers

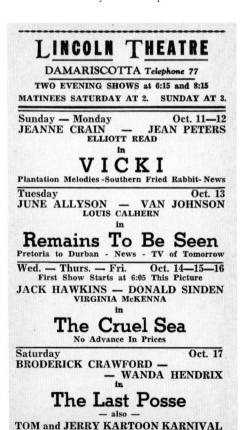
Coming attractions' card, 1953

Photo, June 1994. The Lincoln was originally named Lincoln Hall. Its name was changed to the Lincoln Theatre in the late 1920s

Photo, signboard beside the theatre entrance, June 1994. When I asked Van Reid how good the theatre's "10 people in attendance" batting average has been, he smiled and answered "pretty good."

who have appeared on stage at the Lincoln. And legend has it that it was on that very same stage that *Auld Lang Syne* was first sung in America.

Since 1992 the Lincoln has been operated by the Lincoln County Community Theatre. Thirty-nine year old Van Reid, a member of the L.C.C.T. board of directors, gave me a tour...from the theatre's circa 1935 Simplex Carbon Arc projector to the marvelous 1920 Manley popcorn machine that serves as the lobby's centerpiece. What is wonderfully evident is the L.C.C.T.'s commitment: to both the joy of the theatre's past and to the promise of its future. Restoration - in the style of the 1930s, when the Lincoln enjoyed its original heyday as a movie palace - is very much in progress. Van thinks of the Lincoln as "a rare gem." I think he's right.

Lincoln Theatre
Lincoln

There's the old adage that goes "Don't judge a book by its cover." Add theatres to the old adage. The Lincoln is a prime example. On the outside things are pretty ho hum. On the inside things are quite gorgeous.

The present Lincoln Theatre is the second on the same site. The first was gutted by fire in January of 1922. The second - and present - opened its doors the very next year, 1923. Both were built and owned by the Independent Order of Odd Fellows, with the theatre occupying the first two floors and the Odd Fellows the third and fourth.

The Lincoln has been in business over 70 years. It's a long time. Memories abound. Some people yet recall Warren "Gramp" Butler, who lived to be 106 and who estimated that he saw over 2,300 films at the Lincoln. He died in 1949... but not before he'd been nationally acclaimed as "America's Oldest Movie Fan" in 1946. Then there's 64-year old Lincoln native Avilda McLaughlin. "Every time they changed the show I'd go: I was a real spoiled brat," she laughs. Avilda's all-time favorite is Clark Gable: "He was so handsome." Colleen Tuscan, 68, has fond memories, too. She ought to: she worked at the theatre from 1939 to 1946. Colleen recalls there was a packed house every Saturday... that people would come to town from all around to do their shopping in the afternoon and then they'd go to the picture show at night. Westerns were especially big. Sometimes the place would be mobbed and the projectionist, chortles Colleen, would get the reel on backwards. "The people would roar. They'd think that was hilarious."

Well, Gramp has passed on and Clark Gable hasn't made a movie in awhile and westerns aren't what they used to be... but they're still showing movies at the Lincoln Theatre. The problem is that not many people are coming out to watch them. Peter Quirion, proprietor since 1979, is concerned. "Marginal" is how he describes business. Peter, a 50-year old Bucksport native and former high school history teacher, deserves better. So does the Lincoln. Who cares what's playing. Go to admire the magnificent tin walls and ceiling, the majestic curvaceous - yes, curvaceous! - balcony, and the excellent acoustics. The Lincoln is a showplace!

Photo, September 1994. Apart from its quite splendid original marquee, the exterior of the Lincoln Theatre is not very exciting. Venture inside, however, and you'll find a different story.

Postcard view, circa 1948. Known for steaks, clams, lobster, and homemade pastries and pies, the Lobster House was good enough to earn the coveted "Recommended by Duncan Hines" status. The building to the left was the restaurant's gift shop. "They," recalls Joe Ouellette, "had some good stuff."

THE LOBSTER HOUSE WITH GIFT SHOP APPROVED BY DUNCAN HINES
BAR HARBOR ROAD, TRENTON, ME.   A-46

The Lobster House
Trenton

"It was a good place to eat... the best place I've ever seen around here." Those are the words of 64-year old Joe Ouellette. And he ought to know: he's lived in the Trenton area since the 1940s. He also worked at the Lobster House for five years and recalls "these old ladies that did the cooking" and how good their tenderloin steaks, their hot boiled lobster, and their rum pie was. Joe's older brother, Henry, 71, also worked at the Lobster House, and he, too, has vivid memories. He recalls the homemade blueberry muffins and pecan rolls, fresh vegetables, steamed clams, and, of course, the lobster. And that a lot of notables - Myrna Loy, Ted Williams, Gabby Hayes, Edward Everett Horton, Fess "Davy Crocket" Parker, among others - stopped by at one time or another. Gabby left the most lasting impression: he came right into the kitchen and signed autographs!

The Lobster House was founded by Ellsworth native Dana Mad-docks circa 1937. At first it was on the west side of Route 3. Circa 1940 Dana switched location to the east side and the handsome building pictured here. In 1968 he sold the restaurant to hotel/motel magnate Tom Walsh, who constructed large motel units both behind and adjacent to the restaurant and, in fact, basically ceased operating the restaurant circa 1970. Today the former diners' delight still stands - as part of the Lobster House Motel complex - but is used only for storage and employee lodging.

Lois' Diner
North Berwick

Lois' began life, in 1951, in New Hampshire. It is "from away." It didn't start as Lois', either. The diner, constructed by the Jerry O'Mahony diner manufacturing company of Elizabeth, New Jersey, was originally called the Monarch Diner. It stood at 530 Central Avenue in Dover, New Hampshire. Just who actually owned it is uncertain. Larry Cultrera of Medford, Massachusetts - a man who really knows his diner history - is positive the Monarch was one of a chain of diners owned by the Waltham, Massachusetts-based DeCola Brothers. Dover city directories of the day, however, show Fred and Irene Jewell as the diner's intitial proprietors, followed by Spiros Drakos, and then Erwin Hunt. Most likely the DeColas leased the diner out.

What is certain is that the diner was purchased by North Berwick native Edward Neal in De-cember 1968. Neal's original intention was to convert the diner to a flower shop. "He thought it would be a good place to display flowers," his widow Phyllis recalls. Instead Neal set his new possession in "downtown" North Berwick... and reopened it as a diner that he leased to local chef Lois Griffin.

Lois' operated until late 1973. Lack of parking space, recollects Phyllis, was a major problem. Edward Neal died in January of 1974. His former diner sat vacant until 1986. On March 17th of that year Phyllis had the diner moved to a site next to her greenhouse in Sanford. Phyllis recalls the exact date well, because, she beams, "It was St. Patrick's Day and I wanted to tie a big green bow on top of the diner." But the diner is tall. Phyllis is short. The diner made its trip unadorned.

Since 1986 the former diner has been sitting adjacent to Phyllis' greenhouse, Twombley's, on Twombley Road in Sanford. Phyllis uses it for storage. She says a lot of people have shown interest in the diner... "but they want to give me 10% of what it's worth." Phyllis is in no rush to sell. The diner's old site, to the left of the striking 1893 Commercial block in North Berwick, is now, ironically, a parking lot.

Photo, February 1994

Design, Monarch menu, circa 1955. Service at the Monarch/Lois' isn't what it used to be. The diner, which present-day owner Phyllis Neal refers to as the "Silver Queen," now sits next to her greenhouse in Sanford. It is used for storage.

85

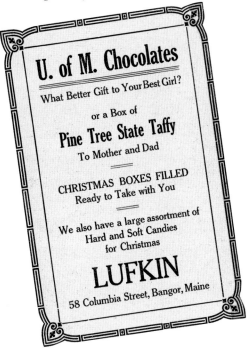

Lufkin's
Bangor

Wonderful memories of Lufkin's abound around Bangor. And for good reason: the shop that George Lufkin founded in 1894 was a sweet-tooth mecca for 67 years. Think of the candy one could eat in 67 years!

George Lufkin was born in Exeter, Maine in 1861. After attending public schools in Exeter and business college in Augusta, he returned to Exeter and ran a general merchandise store. He made the move to Bangor in 1892; the move from general merchandise to candy and confectionery in 1894. Both were good moves.

George's first confectionery shop was located at 14 State Street. By the turn of the century he'd branched out to 13 Park Street and 92 Main Street, and by 1905 he had outlets in Bar Harbor and Castine as well. Eventually, beginning circa 1915, Lufkin centered his operation in the Coe Block on Columbia Street. There he kept six candymakers busy crafting U. of M. Chocolates, Pine Tree Taffy, Almond Butter Krunch, Molasses Kisses, and a host of other goodies. Lufkin's Ice Cream was touted as being second to none, too.

Hilda Warwell, 71, of Bangor, was the first person I asked about Lufkin's. Did she ever light up! "No one else has made butter crunch as well as they did. I've never had any as good since," she assured me (and then added: "although I keep on trying!"). For Dick Stratton, 72, of Hampden, Lufkin's meant Pine Tree Taffy: "They used to sell it on the trains. It came in a little white box. And it *was* tasty." Barbara Baeslack, 67, of Bangor, recalled the caramels as her favorite, but then admitted that's because they were her mother's favorite: "They were always around the house. They were always available." Everyone I spoke with recalled big glass cases and a marble counter and "a very friendly atmosphere."

George Lufkin passed away in 1943. His widow, Eva, took over until she, too, passed away, in 1944. Several different owners then kept the Lufkin's name and tradition alive until 1961, when final proprietor Scott Hathaway decided it was time to call it quits. Sixty-seven years is, after all, a long time.

Ad, 1905... from when Lufkin's was a veritable chain-store operation.

Postcard view, circa 1958.

Ad, November 1948. Mac's was locally famous for both its Thanksgiving and Christmas dinners. Thelma Verrill, who waitressed at the restaurant in the early 1950s, remembers that sometimes it got so busy that people would be lined up outside waiting to get in. Even in the cold.

Mac's Restaurant
Mechanic Falls

Homemade breads. Chicken pie. Boiled dinner on Thursdays. Baked beans on Saturdays. These are the things that people recall about Mac's Restaurant. They recall the pair of bad fires, too: the one in November 1947 and the other in April 1953. But Floyd - who was just about always called "Mac" - McAllister and his wife Beryl rebuilt both times.

Floyd, a 1919 graduate of Mechanic Falls High School, more or less backed into the restaurant business. He always,

in fact, preferred being at his filling station, with Beryl in charge at the restaurant.

The McAllisters sold Mac's in 1967. The new owner, Christine Kyllonen, changed the restaurant's name to Christie's. In early 1969 she also added a gift shop and a cocktail lounge, and remodeled the facade of the entire building. Away went the rather handsome false front and the homey awnings. In came "the modern look."

Floyd McAllister died in October of 1968. Beryl moved to Florida where she passed away sometime thereafter. Christine Kyllonen operated Christie's until 1987. It's now called Sharon's Restaurant and Captain's Pub. Any resemblance between it and the photo of Mac's shown here is purely coincidental.

Magic Lantern Theatre
Bridgton

How many theatres in Maine can you think of that have had six different names during their run at the box office? I can think of but one, and that one, of course, is the theatre that we now know as the Magic Lantern.

Name number one was the New Meserve, in honor of Claude Meserve, who owned the building in which the theatre opened in June of 1929. Two more names - the Meserve, and the New Bridgton - followed before the name Mayfair was adopted. The Mayfair's grand opening took place April 22, 1935. Admission was 10¢ for children, 25¢ for adults, and - on opening night only - there were free flowers for the first 75 ladies to show up with 25¢ in hand.

The theatre lasted almost two decades as the Mayfair. Its most momentous event occurred in March of 1942: a fire swept through the top of the theatre building, causing extensive damage to the third floor. Previously used as a roller skating rink, the floor was unoccupied at the time. What was left was lopped off and never rebuilt. What had been a three-story structure became a two-story structure.

In January of 1954 the Mayfair closed its doors. Five months later, however, it was reopened as the Brookside under new

Ad, May 1935. The theatre that is today the Magic Lantern was called the Mayfair from 1935 until 1954.

Two Shows 7 & 9 | **MAYFAIR THEATRE Bridgton, Me** | **Daylight Time**

FRIDAY & SATURDAY
King Vidor's Masterpiece
"OUR DAILY BREAD"
starring KAREN MORELY
— CO-FEATURE —
JOHN WAYNE
IN
"THE MAN FROM UTAH"
A Blue Streak of Action—Adventure

MON. - TUES. MAY 27 - 28
Here It Is!
JAMES CAGNEY
In a New Role—Singing & Dancing
His Way Thru
"FOOTLIGHT PARADE"
WITH
Ruby Keeler — Joan Blondell
GUY KIBBEE

WED. & THURS. — MAY 29 & 30
Presenting
Louisa M. Alcott's
IMMORTAL CLASSIC
" *Little Men* "
RALPH MORGAN — ERIN O'BRIEN — MOORE
SPECIAL: Children's 10¢ Mat., Wed. 3:30 P. M. — Thurs., Reg. Mat. 2:30

owner Everett Douglass. More than just the name had changed: Douglass had taken the five months to almost completely do over the theatre. New was a marquee, central entrance, redecorated lobby, paneled walls, new lighting, new chairs, new restrooms, and a new sound system. The old theatre was a new theatre!

Brookside was the theatre's longest-running name. John Tevanian, who now owns and operates the Bridgton Drive-In (q.v.) even managed it from 1971 through the end of the summer season in 1976. A man named Tommy Goodman then came into the picture. It was he

who gave the theatre name number six. He called it the Magic Lantern. He also upgraded the interior and installed a Dolby Sound System. Highlights during Goodman's years at the helm included a pair of "almost" premieres. Former Bridgton resident Stephen King arranged to have his 1980 movie *The Shining* shown at the Magic Lantern a full two days before it was viewed in virtually all of the rest of the country. Proceeds went to benefit the Northern Cumberland Memorial Hospital. And in November of 1982, King again came through for the folks in Bridgton, with his *Creepshow* making its southern Maine debut at the Magic Lantern.

Well, the old theatre is in its mid-sixties now. Old enough to retire and collect social security. For a time it appeared as if that's just what would happen. Tommy Goodman closed the Magic Lantern in 1985. The Bridgton Recreation Department ran it for one summer season. The theatre then sat idle until 1988, when local businessman Clarence Howell and his family took over and made things happen again. They converted the theatre to a twin in 1990. No longer was it just seasonal, either: since 1990 the Magic Lantern has been open all year, featuring family-quality movies, low admission, and a funky - complete with a working player piano - lobby. The management team of Shirley Howell, her son Peter, and daughter Elizabeth, clearly enjoys the theatre. As Elizabeth was only too happy to tell me: "I like making people feel at home; I love working here."

Photo, June 1994. Located at 69 Main Street, the theatre building was three stories high until 1942. A fire in March of that year changed that, however. The third floor was so badly damaged that it was removed. The building has been two stories ever since.

Photo, lobby sign, June 1994. Take your pick: since 1990 the Magic Lantern has been a twin.

Main Street, Maine

I like Main Street. I like the brick and stone buildings. And the wooden ones, too. I like it that there are tall buildings and short buildings; thin buildings and fat buildings. I like the fact that many of the buildings have been around a long time. Age builds character.

I like it that most of the stores and restaurants are locally owned and not part of a chain owned by someone in New Jersey or California or Kansas City. And, most of all, I like the fact that every Main Street is different from every other Main Street.

You're neat, Main Street.

Postcard view, circa 1935

Postcard view, circa 1945

90

Postcard views, circa 1945-1950.
If you get half the chance, take a
drive - or, better yet, a walk -
down some or all of these main
streets... and see if you don't
agree they still look pretty
darned good these many years
later.

Mary's Candy Shop
Lewiston

When I suggested to Lucille Meservier, co-proprietor of Mary's Candy Shop, that there are people who would almost kill for her job, she laughed. "It's funny," she said, "when you work in it - candy and chocolate - all the time it gets to be something you don't crave. You crave something different." But Lucille - along with her husband and co-proprietor, Armand - does love what she does. She likes the people she meets as customers, and she likes creating recipes for new concoctions. She's also very proud that she and Armand are carrying on a tradition and craft that goes back to 1933. That's the year Greek immigrant Jimmy Lafkiotes set up Mary's Candy Shop at 235 Main Street. He

Photo, October 1994. Lucille and Armand take time off from candymaking to pose for the camera.

Photo by Sharon Packer, Auburn.

Package design, 1994. The location of Mary's Candy Shop may have changed but its most attractive box design sure hasn't. Lucille is almost certain that the design she's using today goes all the way back to 1933.

named the shop for his wife and co-worker, Mary.

Jim and Mary Lafkiotes ran their shop for a hefty 23 years, retiring in 1956 when he was 63 and she was 49. The new owner was Joe Groleau. He was a man well qualified to carry on: he'd worked at Mary's for eight years prior to his purchase of the operation.

The third and present owner of Mary's, coincidentally, also worked there eight years before becoming proprietor. That's Lucille. She and Armand - a for-

mer loomfixer at the Bates Mill - bought out Joe in 1979. Their biggest challenge came in 1982. Their lease at 235 Main (which now, much remodeled, is home to Century 21 Brickel, Kilbreth, & Tierney Realty) was running out. Armand and Lucille didn't want to move but realized that there was little choice. Fortune smiled, however. What had been the Asian Food Store, located diagonally across Main Street at number 238, became available. The Meserviers knew it was the right move. Their "new" location - on the first floor of a handsome

92

Midway Drive-In Theatre
Detroit

You'd have to admit that June 1955 was a banner month for the Newport/Pittsfield area. The largest Tastee Freeze in the State of Maine opened in Newport. The president of the United States, Dwight D. Eisenhower, visited Pittsfield. And the Midway Drive-In Theatre sprang into operation midway between the two, in Detroit.

The grand opening of the drive-in was Thursday, June 16th. Admission was 50¢ for adults. "Kiddies" were free. On the screen - "one of Maine's largest and finest cinemascope screens," lauded *The Pittsfield Advertiser* - was Alfred Hitchcock's *Rear Window*, starring Grace Kelly and James Stewart, and George Montgomery in *The Lone Gun*.

The Midway's stated goal was "to give the surrounding communities the best in shows, food, and service." No one could dispute the theatre's success in achieving that goal at first. Rocky Connors, 70, of Pittsfield remembers taking his whole family to the drive-in on many an occassion. His kids liked the playground. He liked the fact that the grounds were kept clean and well-maintained. Newport-native Don Hallenbeck, 37, was a kid when he went to the Midway. He, too, recalls the playground (especially, as he puts it, "the obligatory swing set"). And

circa 1895 five-story brick building - has been a boon to Lucille and Armand. For one thing, it's bigger than the original shop. For another, it's in a more visible spot. Mostly, though, it may be they're just that much better able to do their own thing in a shop where no other candymaker has trod before. Lucille exhilarates as she discusses original creations such as peach creams and rum-flavored cherry Needhams. She naturally has a fondness for the shop's bestsellers, too: yum yums (caramel and pecans coated on one side with milk chocolate; on the other with dark chocolate), almond butter crunch, and just good old regular Needhams. Interestingly, she says it's the ladies who really go for "the sweet things," the hand-dipped chocolates and fudge. She estimates that 80% of her chocolate sales are accounted for by women. Men are much more apt to head for the salted nut display case.

But back to Lucille's own personal fondness. Her own personal taste temptation. "My weakness is pastry," she admits as her eyes light up. "Pies and cakes and cookies and turnovers," she enumerates. And her eyes light up even more.

that it was very well kept. But Don also recalls that the Midway became the "Ill-Repute Theatre," a theatre that showed mostly x-rated pictures. That was in the mid-to-late 1970s. Skowhegan-native Lisa Nelson, 31, admits to having gone to the theatre during its "ill-repute" days. She was 17 or so and went with her boyfriend: "It was where I saw my first x-rated movie. I was shocked." And Lisa's boyfriend... how did he react? "He loved it," Lisa laughs, "but, then again, he suggested it."

After a while the steady stream of x-rated shows got to the people of Detroit. Some of them, anyway. First selectman Joe Schissler recalls that "We had

The drive-in,
spring.

It's difficult to find photos of drive-ins when they were in their heyday. People went and saw and enjoyed for years... but very few people bothered to take a photograph. All three of these photos are courtesy of Joyce and Delbert McLaggan of Detroit. But even these shots of the Midway, taken in 1969-1970, are not really of the theatre per se: the McLaggans lived across Route 100 from the drive-in and took these photos of their family. The Midway just happened to be there in the background.

The drive-in,
summer

The drive-in,
winter

Courtesy of Frank
Woodworth, Detroit.

people coming in (to town hall)
and complaining that the theatre
was showing porn movies."
They got up a petition. Finally,
no one recollects exactly when,
the town passed an anti-
obscenity ordinance, geared to
get the Midway to either close
down or mend its "evil ways."

Between pressure from the town
and ever-increasing competition
from television and video
rentals, the Midway wound
down. It finally closed after the
1985 season. By that time, states
Joe Schissler, "There was ab-
solutely no financial return."

Part of the Midway remains
standing. That part is the former
concession stand/projection
building. You can see it, looking
rather forlorn, about 2.2 miles
east of Pittsfield on routes 11
and 100. It's on the right side,
just before Frank Woodworth's
contracting company.

Miller's Tourist Box Lunch
Woolwich

A place to get a bite to eat, gas
up the car, and rent a cabin for
the night, too... such was Herbert T. Miller and Alton P. Reed's
contribution to the world from
circa 1928 to circa 1932.
Records are sketchy, but it
appears that Miller, a native of
California, and Reed, a native of
Woolwich, teamed up to provide
roadside's basic amenities for
about five years, then sold to
Mrs. Lulu Atkins. She operated
the complex - under the name
Hillcrest Cabins - until 1935 or
so. The various buildings, in the
words of local history maven
Burnette Wallace, then "more or
less disappeared."

Herbert T. Miller eventually
moved back to California. Alton
P. Reed, who owned a number of
stores in the Bath/George-
town/Woolwich area during his
lifetime, died in Bath at age 87
in 1976. The site of the partners'
former endeavor on what is now
George Wright Road/old U.S.
Route 1 is today occupied by a
private residence.

P.S. Alton P. Reed's son, Walter, 82, still
operates a one-pump station on George
Wright Road, the old Route 1/Atlantic
Highway, in Woolwich. Why not stop by,
admire the aged Orange Crush ad hang-
ing in his station, and give him a little
business? Things have been slow since
the road in front of the station ceased to
be Route 1.

Courtesy of Historic Preservation Commission, Augusta.

Postcard view, circa 1930.

Photo, circa 1950. The Miss Aroostook stood at 9 Bangor Street/Union Square, about where the Dallas Henderson State Farm agency is now.

Courtesy of Dana Cheney, Monticello.

Every year tourists who stop at Miss Aroostook Diner tell the folks there how they have eaten there before and have looked forward to coming back, sometimes driving out of their way to call. This makes Glen Philbrick, the rotund owner happy and you will be happy too if you lunch or dine at the - -

Ad, 1957

MISS AROOSTOOK DINER
Union Square

Miss Aroostook Diner
Houlton

The Miss Aroostook was a "Worcester," manufactured by the Worcester Lunch Car Company of Worcester, Massachusetts, and by all accounts it was a beauty. Bright blue and yellow on the outside; sparkling and shiny and adorned with a marble counter on the inside. It started up on Monday, November 24, 1947, was open seven days a week from 5:00 AM to midnight, featured a Rockola jukebox, and promised full course meals, short order lunches, and special Sunday dinners.

The diner lived up to its promise. "A good place to stop: good coffee, good doughnuts,

cheerful service." That's how 67-year old Bruce Burnham remembers the Miss Aroostook. Mary Suitter, 65, is even more emphatic. "Damned good food": those are her words.

The Miss Aroostook's initial proprietor was Glen Philbrick. After a dozen years, in 1959, he sold to Dana Cheney. Cheney had learned the restaurant trade by operating eateries in both Caribou and Presque Isle before further honing his skills closer to home in Houlton. His first ven-

ture was Dana's Food Store on Market Square. His second was the Miss Aroostook. Operating both, however, eventually proved to be too much: Dana Cheney closed the diner circa 1972. Today part of the Miss Aroostook exists. It is attached to the side of a bar and grill and pool hall known as Mum's, at 142 Military Road. You'll recognize the familiar arched roof, and the tile floor. But you won't recognize anything else.

Photo, December 1994.

Miss Portland Diner
Portland

By last count there are four places in Portland that call themselves "diner." But there's only one that's a *real* diner. To be *real*, in the eyes of diner buffs, a diner must have been built by a diner manufacturing company and then transported to its site. Portland's one *real* diner is, of course, the Miss Portland. And 70-year old Jimmie Crowder, now of South Portland, well recalls its manufacture, in 1949. He should: he was 25-year old Jimmie Crowder then... and he was the Miss Portland's co-proprietor. "We (Jimmie and Frank Venuti, his partner) wanted to start a business. We figured a diner would be a good thing for

the Portland area," Jimmie says. The partners had heard about the now legendary diner maker, the Worcester Lunch Car Company, motored on down to Worcester, and were treated royally. "They took us all through the plant," Jimmie still recalls vividly. "It was amazing the way they (the diners) came off the line." Impressed, Jimmie and Frank decided it was a Worcester for them. "They had quite a few models," Jimmie continues. "We chose one (the $37,000 model) and it came, via flatbed, a month or so later." Jimmie and Frank had the foundation waiting. "All we did was unload the diner, jack it up, put it on the foundation, and hook up the water and sewer lines." Voila, instant diner! The grand open-

ing was March 7, 1949. Ads promised "Maine's Largest and Most Modern Streamlined Diner."

When it was new to town, the Miss Portland stood at 175 Forest Avenue. Jimmie and Frank called it the Miss Portland because "We wanted the name to say Portland." Business was good. "We were busy all the time, night and day." The partners even contemplated opening a second diner. A Miss Portland II, if you will. Before that could happen, however, the partnership began to unravel. Jimmie recalls that Frank started to gamble. "Then it (the business) started to go downhill." In 1954 Jimmie and Frank sold to brothers Myer and Harry Marcus. Next in line of proprietors was Harold Foley and Al Karas. They bought in 1964, the same year the Miss Portland was moved to its present location at 49 Marginal Way. The move was necessitated by the construction of the Federal Building on what had been the diner's site.

Randy Chasse took over as the Miss Portland's proud proprietor in April 1981. Fourteen years later he's still proprietor. And he's still proud. You could even say that owning the Miss Portland has been his life's ambition. When Randy was a youngster, about 5 or 6, his dad was a sausagemaker for Auburn Packing. All these years later -

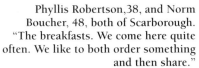

What brings folks to the 45-year old classic they call the Miss Portland? I asked an assortment of people one Friday morning. Here's what they said.

Phyllis Robertson,38, and Norm Boucher, 48, both of Scarborough. "The breakfasts. We come here quite often. We like to both order something and then share."

Bill Gray, Jr., 59, Portland. "The oatmeal. I'm an oatmeal kind of guy. They (the waitresses) see me driving up and get the oatmeal ready."

Eli Heakin, 8, Portland. "The pancakes." Eli was dining with his mother, Bonnie: "We like to stop at the Miss Portland before I go to work and Eli goes to school. We do it every couple of weeks. It's a treat."

L to r, Sue Dakers, 30, Portland, Diane Lee, 34, Portland, and Bonnie Wood, 42, New Gloucester. "Work. We work here." Diane spoke for the trio: "I love it (working at the diner). I love the people and all the different types of people."

Randy's now 52 - he recalls "I used to see a lot of orders going to the Miss Portland Diner." It made a lasting impression. When the chance to buy the diner came along, Randy didn't hesitate to take it.

What Randy is proudest of is "the interest in the place." By that he means the video-makers who have used the diner as a backdrop (the Maine State Lottery and LaVerdiere's, among others) and, especially, its inclusion in Mel Gibson's movie, *Man Without a Face*. He's also proud of the diner's food. Then again, he should be: he cooks most of it! It's not just the taste, though: it's, in Randy's words, "the nutritional value and emphasis on low fat" as well.

In spite of it all, however, Randy has a desire to sell the Miss Portland and move on to something else. In late 1993/early 1994 he held a "Write-An-Essay-And-Send-In-$100.00 Contest." It didn't work. "There was a lot of interest but not enough essays" is how Randy puts it. What's down the road for the Miss Portland is uncertain, but one thing's for sure and that's Randy's pledge that he won't sell unless it's to the "right" owner: an owner who'll, again in his words, "maintain the diner's integrity. I don't," he states emphatically, "want it to change."

All photos, December 1994.

Coming attractions
folder, 1940.

movie and vaudeville fare to
Sagadahoc County. A man who
remembers well the glory days
of the Opera House is 68-year
old Bath native Donald Povich.
He, in fact, saw his very first
movie at the Opera House. It
was circa 1935, and it was a
shoot-'em-up starring Tom Mix.
Donald still recalls a scene
where Tom, while perched atop
a peaked roof, roped one of the
bad guys. Donald can also still
recall the theatre's curtain: "It
was blue and purple and had a
large oval with a painting of a
seascape." He and his pals liked
to sit in the balcony. "It was
some kind of thrill to sit up
there!" And that's right where he
was, in the a balcony's first row,
on the eve of December 7, 1941.
On the screen was the Gary
Cooper classic, *Sergeant York*,

when the manager stopped the
movie, walked on stage, and
announced "The Japanese have
attacked Pearl Harbor and
Manila." Then the movie continued. But somehow it wasn't the
same. Although only 15, Donald
knew the score. He turned to a
balconymate and simply said "I
think we're in a war."

The Opera House survived
World War II and then postwar
expansion. But it couldn't sur-
vive TV. Donald recalls that
toward the end "The theatre got
shabby and the movies got
sleazy." The Opera House closed
on December 1, 1970. It was
demolished the following
November. On the site there is
now a parking lot.

Pastime Theatre
Brunswick

For almost five decades the Pastime Theatre was a mecca for
Brunswick-area moviegoers.
Constructed and originally managed by Wallace O. Gould, the
Pastime opened for business in
March 1908. Ads promised
safety ("Large Exits Opening
Outward"/"Picture Machine Fire
Proof") and propriety ("We cater
to ladies, gentlemen, and children. None others"). An early
1909 announcement promised a
Free One-Year Pass for the
woman "whom our patrons
declare is the Most Beautiful
Lady in Brunswick."

Never as elegant as its nearby

Courtesy of Pejepscot Historical Society, Brunswick.

Photo, circa 1928. There was an added treat
in going to the Pastime: next door was a
candy store. Long known as The Quality
Shop and later The Kandy Kitchen, the
shop was a must either before or after the
show. The Kandy Kitchen's homemade
peanut butter bon bons are said to have
been especially good.

cousin, the Cumberland Theatre (opened in 1912), the Pastime was basic. No frills. "It wasn't fancy. It was plain. The seats were plain. There was no fancy stage." That's how 73-year old Betty Hyde describes the Pastime. But her eyes light up as she recalls that the theatre "ran a serial every week... and got you going so you'd have to go again the next week." Then there were the great old Westerns. That's what 70-year old Harry A. Alexander, Jr. remembers most from his youth in the early 1930s and 1940s: Gene Autry, Hopalong Cassidy, the Three Musketeers. Ride 'em, Brunswick cowboy!

By the 1950s, though, the Pastime was hurting. It closed in July of 1955. The reason, stated manager John Peabody, was "competition from television and outdoor theatres."

The former theatre sat vacant for six years before being demolished in 1961. Its site at 149 Maine Street is today occupied by the entrance to and a parking lot for the Tontine Mall.

Pat's Pizza
Orono

I wouldn't call Pat Farnsworth a legend. But I would call him a pretty famous guy. After all, who else can you think of that has 16 pizza places named after him? Yet, in spite of all his success, Pat remains unassuming, just a man who likes to wear white shirts and red suspenders and enjoys a good cigar.

Carl Douglas "Pat" Farnsworth was born in Harrington, Maine in 1909. His family moved to Orono when he was two. Pat and Orono have gotten along very well since. Pat graduated from Orono High School in 1928. While in school he worked weekends as a clerk at George King's Ice Cream, Confectionary, and Fruit Store on Orono's Mill Street. It was a job that would profoundly affect his life. In 1929 George King went bankrupt. "He lost everything in the (stock market) crash," Pat

recalls. Several proprietors tried their hand at the store. None could make it work. In July of 1931, now all of 21, Pat was working with his dad, a chef at the Lookout Hotel in Ogunquit, when he received a phone call. Was he interested in buying the store? It didn't take him long to decide "Why not?!" So with $75.00 back pay and $100.00 his father loaned him, Pat headed back to Orono... and the world of eventual big business.

Renamed the C.D. Farnsworth Ice Cream Parlor/Farnsworth's Cafe, Pat's endeavor started slowly... and continued that way for the next 22 years. Full-course meals were added in 1933, with Pat's mother, Eva, doing most of the cooking. Beer was added when the nation went wet again in 1933. And Pat remodeled the place in 1945. Nothing seemed to make much difference. Business was lacklustre. "We were struggling," Pat admits.

Courtesy of Pat Farnsworth, Orono

Photo, circa 1935. Pat, looking dapper on the left, and employees Irene Goodin, Joyce King, and Bill Courthers pose in front of Pat's ice cream parlor and cafe. Pat remodeled in 1945. Not much has changed architecturally since then. The result is a feeling of warmth. Downright comfortable warmth. There's 11 red-topped stools, 11 booths (no, 11 is not Pat's lucky number), an old stand-up wooden telephone booth, individual jukebox selection boxes, and a very-well worn countertop. There's no way that countertop, however, is going to be resurfaced as long as Pat is running things. As he says: "Think of how many elbows it took to make it like it is."

Circa 1951 a new owner took over at the former University Inn around the corner from Pat's and turned it into a pizza parlor. Pizza was new to Maine at the time. No big deal, figured Pat. "We thought pizzas were a flash in the pan... that they wouldn't amount to anything," he says, cracking a smile. After awhile, though, pizzas got him annoyed. Not that people *were eating* pizzas... but that they *were eating* them in *his* place. "My customers would sit in my tap room and use my phone and call up the pizza place, order a pizza and then get it and bring it back and eat it." Enough is enough, Pat finally realized: "If you can't lick 'em, join 'em!"

As it turned out, though, *deciding* to add pizza was one thing. Being able to *actually do it* was another. Pizza parlors were few and far between in those pizza prehistoric days. Pat eventually discovered Angelone's in Portland, contacted proprietor John Angelone, and was told, "Sure, come on down and I'll show you (how to make pizza)." Pat's wife, Frances, made the trip and she stayed ten days. "He taught her everything, and he didn't charge us a cent," Pat says appreciatively.

The rest can only be called history. On his first day in the pizza business Pat recalls that he said "If I sell 50 pizzas today I'll be happy." He sold over 100, and was very happy. Today, between himself and his son Bruce, he sells over 350,000 a year, and is even happier. To what does Pat attribute his success? "Word of mouth advertising," he says... but then admits "They had to like the pizza to start with."

105

PETTENGILL'S OPERA HOUSE, ISLAND FALLS, ME. 20K.

Courtesy of Maine Historic Preservation Commission, Augusta

Pettengill's Opera House
Island Falls

Now 57, Oakfield-native Donna James recalls the days when "We thought we were in seventh heaven when we came to Island Falls" and the movies at Pettengill's Opera House. Well, if 74-year old Agnes Maxfield has her way, coming to Island Falls will, some year soon, again be a trip to seventh heaven.

Built in 1894, what became Pettengill's Opera House was originally a general store and hall. The general store was downstairs and the hall was upstairs. The owner was C.L. (Columbus Lamb) Pettengill, a Vanceboro native who'd made a heap of money in the lumber business. Through the years the hall was used for a variety of functions. Plays, dances, church and school gatherings, recitals, basketball: you name it and it probably took place at Pettengill's Hall somewhere along the way. But moving pictures became the staple... and by the mid-1920s "Pettengill's Hall" had become "Pettengill's Opera House." Clayton Varney, 71, recalls there'd be four shows a week, on Monday, Friday, and Saturday evenings, plus, of course, a Saturday matinee. Clayton can also recall when sound came to the Opera House in the 1930s. At first, he says, he thought sound was a novelty. "But then," he adds, "I figured it was here to stay."

C.L.'s son, Bert, took over the Opera House in the early 1920s. And *his* son, Carl, eventually took over and ran operations until 1965 or so. I asked Carl, now 95, why he finally closed down. He replied that by the mid-1960s "it didn't pay" to run the theatre anymore: "We just had kids and they didn't come to see the movie. They came to throw things."

Enter Agnes Maxfield. A graduate of Island Falls High School - "I graduated from the Opera House stage in 1938," she states proudly - Agnes is out to restore Pettengill's. "This is my project," she declares. "I loved this building. It was the center of everything."

Will Agnes, a retired registered nurse who purchased the building in 1989, succeed? I sincerely hope so. The building has seen better days, but all the ingredients - gorgeous wall and ceiling murals, wainscoting, most of the 300 seats, etc. - are there. "Come back in another year and you won't know the place," she told me. I believe her.

The Pier
Old Orchard Beach

Most of the headlines in southern Maine's newspapers that July of 1898 were about the war with Spain, but they could just as well have been about the opening of the Great Steel Pier at Old Orchard Beach. Ads touted the Pier as the "Coney Island of New England," declared that - at 1,900 feet - it was the longest pier in the world, and boasted it was capable of holding 20,000 people. Opening day, July 2, was marked by the arrival of all six New England governors, a Grand Promenade, music galore, and fireworks that the *Biddeford Daily Times* described as "a beautiful spectacle as they cast their scintillating radiance over the dark water below."

Almost a century later the Pier still seldom fails to satisfy. Not that today's Pier is the same structure that was so lauded in 1898. No, in fact, today's Pier is actually something like Pier #5. The first Pier - the "Coney Island of New England" - enchanted visitors for just a little over a decade before it was mauled by a winter storm in late March of 1909. The end of the Pier somehow survived. The section closest to shore did, too. But the middle 500 feet floated out to sea, never to be seen again. The Pier was, of course, put together again, but the end result was a greatly shortened model. Nevertheless, it was this Pier - Pier #2 - that saw the landmark enjoy its greatest glory. Spearheaded by English-immigrant John Duffy, who took over as owner in 1913, the Pier featured name bands from one end of summer to the other. And everybody danced! A 1923 ad said it all:

Pier, Old Orchard Beach, Maine

Published in Germany for G. W. Morris, Portland, Maine.

Postcard view, circa 1905, showing the original Pier... all 1,900 feet of it!

Old Orchard Beach Pier after the great Storm of March 25, 1909.

Postcard view, 1909. Oops. The great storm of 1909 didn't do the original Pier any favors.

"Dance O'er the Waves." (And added, for good measure: "Yes! We Have No Mosquitoes!"). Glenn Miller, Benny Goodman, Duke Ellington, Rudy Vallee, the Dorseys, Stan Kenton, Ozzie Nelson, Ella Fitzgerald, Artie Shaw, Guy Lombardo, Buddy Morrow:

View of the Pier at Old Orchard Beach, Maine — D-36

Casino and Pier at Night. Old Orchard Beach, Me.

Postcard views, 1930 (left) and circa 1950 (above). Everybody who was anybody played the Pier!

they all played the Casino at the Pier! By the mid-1950s, though, the era of the big band was on the wane. Rock 'n roll moved in and the dancing went on until 1959, when it became cost ineffective to hire live bands. A storm ended even the dream of those musical heydays when it blew away the Casino in 1972.

Yet another storm, in February 1978, chipped away at the Pier when it demolished 200 feet of its walkway. It was a big "chip": the Pier, what was left of it, was closed down. It remained closed for two seasons while its future was weighed and reweighed. Finally, in June of 1980, a new Pier was - yet again - unveiled. At 400 feet in length it was considerably shorter than old number 1... but it was still the Pier.

Postcard view, circa 1910. Long before there was "Where's Waldo?" there was Old Orchard Beach.

$5.00 Reward if you find me in this crowd of bathers at Old Orchard Beach, Me..

Posed souvenir postcard, 1921

THE MOUNTAINS ARE FINE BUT OLD ORCHARD FOR MINE 1921

As then-governor Joe Brennan, on hand for the opening festivities, said: "Old Orchard Beach has not been Old Orchard Beach without a Pier. Now it is Old Orchard Beach again."

All postcards except circa 1905 and circa 1940 views courtesy of Maine Historic Preservation Commission, Augusta.

ENTRANCE TO THE PIER, OLD ORCHARD BEACH, MAINE.   106365

Courtesy of Rick Poore, Standish

Postcard view, left, showing the entrance to the Pier circa 1940, and photo, June 1995, showing it now. It's still quite a place.

Pineland Diner
Augusta

It is said that travel is broadening. If so, then the Pineland Diner can certainly be considered "broadened," for what was once tabbed "Maine's Most Modern Diner" has become "Maine's Most Moved Diner."

Harris Ellis began it all. He opened the Pineland in 1938-1939. Business was good and Harry's sister-in-law Jeannette Blake joined the Pineland team as co-proprietor during the war years. By 1948 Harry, himself, had left to become chef at the Blaine Restaurant on Water Street, leaving the diner in charge of his wife Loretta and her brother, Leon Page. By 1955, Leon was sole proprietor, and so he would remain for the remainder of the Pineland's days in Augusta, through 1970.

Looking back, people seem to recall the warmth of the Pineland as much as they recall the food. Eighty-five year old Dan Hickey remembers that "there was always a very compatible group of people there," while 66-year old Paul Gregoire recalls "a lot of laughs; everyone was real friendly."

The laughs ceased circa 1970. Dan Hickey's theory is that Leon and his crew just plain wore out: all that getting up in the morning at 4:00 AM day-in-day-out, seven days a week, got to them. He's probably right. In any case, Leon Page took a job with the VA hospital at Togus and closed the diner. Where the diner stood at 181 State Street is now a parking lot between Cumberland Farms and the building that houses Dube Travel Agency.

New adventures, however, were in store for the Pineland. Within a year or so the diner was moved to Waldoboro where it sat in storage until it was moved to Northport by new owner Wendy Leary. There she refurbished it and operated it as a more-or-less gourmet restaurant in the late 1970s. Then it was time to move again, this time to Ellsworth. The man who bought the diner, Michael Palmer, decided that what "The Friendly City" needed was an upscale diner. "Gourmet Fare in an Art Deco Setting," phrased a 1984 brochure. Palmer's endeavor, which he named Michael's Pineland Diner, began in the summer of 1982 and lasted until 1988 or so. Then it folded.

Ad, 1941. Steak and lobster for sure. But what Paul Gregoire remembers most is the breakfasts he'd get at the Pineland. He chuckles when he recounts an incident from 1959 or so: "I recall I went in there one morning and sat next to a big guy. He must have weighed 250-260. He was having a couple of muffins and a cup of coffee. I ordered eggs, home fries, toast, coffee, juice and a couple of doughnuts. The big guy looked at me - I weighed all of 160 - and exclaimed, 'It ain't always the big guy who eats the most.'"

...and Maidee's
Cafe International
Ellsworth

But the idea of an upscale diner in Ellsworth lived on. Rob Rule, who came to Ellsworth via New Jersey, and Maidee Chang, who came via Taiwan and New York, bought the Pineland and made it the core of their dream... a "regular" restaurant wrapped around the diner. They spent months shaping and renovating the diner. Bob Haslam, Jr. was there. Bob, who's 38 and who's been with Rob and Maidee since "the beginning," remembers taking down the Pineland's orange and black wall tiles (with the black shaped like pine trees). "They were falling apart and couldn't be matched up," he says, somewhat dolefully. Bob also recalls that when the Pineland was first covered over, in 1989, a lot of townspeople said "What a shame: they took away the diner."

Well, they didn't, of course. It was reborn as the lounge for what Rob and Maidee named Maidee's Cafe International. Does it yet look like a diner? Yep. Does it say "Pineland Diner" anymore? Yep, too. But only if you go into the kitchen and poke around:

the original porcelain-over-metal nameplate panels are there, preserved but hidden.

One last question and answer. Can a 1930s' diner from Augusta, Maine find happiness in a 1990s' semi-posh Chinese and American restaurant in Ellsworth, Maine?

Yes, I think it can.

Photos, both
November 1994.

The outside... and the inside. Hey, there's a diner in here! When patrons first notice the diner, says bartender Sally Furrow, "They're amused. And they come around and look it over." What they'll also notice is a variety of "wise" sayings above the bar. Everyone who works at Maidee's gets together and helps dream them up. My favorite: "Confucius Say: No Payee, No Drinkee, Not Even Sippee."

111

Circa 1930 postcard view. That's "Old Mom" Goff in front of her tea room. Ridlonville is the former name for a section of eastern Mexico.

Courtesy of Maine Historic Preservation Commission, Augusta

Pine Grobe Tea Room, Ridlonbille Maine

Pine Grove Tea Room
Mexico

Tea rooms - restaurants that served "dainty" meals in quaint surroundings - were all the rage in the 1920s. Mexico was not to be denied. Mrs. Harriet Goff saw to that: circa 1925 she took over what had been a small ice cream/cold drink business and turned it into a full-fledged dining room. She did all the cooking, and it was good. Longtime neighbor, 66-year old Frances DeFillip, recalls that Mrs. Goff "put out a beautiful chicken dinner." Frances also recalls that Mrs. Goff did not possess the world's sweetest disposition. "Old Mom" was her nickname. She and her husband Gene had constructed five overnight cabins and things would flare when

"Old Mom" squared off with Fred Weeks, proprietor of the just-across-the-road Birchwood Cabins. As cars approached and slowed down the two of them would harangue over whose cabins were better. Frances and her family would sit on their porch and take it all in. "It was pretty exciting," she laughs.

The Goffs sold the Pine Grove to Harry and Urania Vail and Urania's sister Evelyn, and her husband, Ray Smart, in 1938. The Vails operated until Harry's death in 1969. In the years since, Urania sold off the cabins, tore down the old tea room building, and moved to a nursing home. On the Pine Grove's former site, 281 River Road/Route 2, there is today a small residence.

Portland Drive-In Theatre
Scarborough

When it opened on July 2, 1949 the Portland Drive-In was big news. For good reason. It was only the second ozoner - as drive-ins were sometimes called - in the entire state.* And it was huge, with a 1,000-car capacity and a screen that measured 70

Ad, June 1968. Later that year the Portland Drive-In would become the Portland Twin Drive-In.

feet by 60 feet. The Portland *Evening Express*, in fact, hailed the theatre as "easily the largest of its kind in the East," and as possessing "the largest movie screen in the Country." Admission was 50¢ per person. Cars were free. And so were children under 12. The kids had their own special playground, too. It was all part of the appeal. As the theatre's opening evening ads sang out: "No More Baby Sitter Problem!" Bring the whole family.

By 1953 it was estimated that the nation's drive-ins were doing a solid 25% of the country's total movie business. The Portland Drive-In was right there doing its share. And it did so all through the fifties. The sixties, too. Business was so brisk, in fact, that a second drive-in was added in October of 1968. The Portland Drive-In became the Portland Twin Drive-In!

Eventually, of course, hard times came to town. Cable TV, VCR, and multi-screen indoor cinemas

all took their toll. In a 1982 article in *Portland Chronicle* magazine, David Priest, district manager for SBC Management, a Somersville, Massachusetts' firm that owned the Portland Twin, stated flat-out the "The Drive-In will never be what it used to be."

How right he was. The Portland Twin fell prey to smaller and smaller turnouts, until the end came in 1986. In September of that year it showed its last double features - *Bullies* and *The Money Pit* on the West screen; *The Karate Kid II* and *Murphy's Romance* on the East - and then rode into the Scarborough sunset.

*The Saco Open Air Auto Theatre, later the Saco Auto Theatre, now the Saco Drive-In, was the first. It opened way back in 1939.

Ad, July 1958. For the better part of two decades, from the mid-1950s to circa 1973, the Portland Drive-In doubled as a church. As explained by Jim Boody, who's been with First Baptist for over 35 years: "It was an attempt to reach people that would not otherwise come through the (church) door."

Both photos, 1990.

The theatre closed in 1986. But its memorable sign remained. Scarborough town councilor Janice Peltier tried to save it; local sign company owner Joe Tufts agreed to help. But their efforts were to no avail: the sign was demolished in late March, 1994.

Quick Service Cafe
Norway

"Quick service" is probably not what one would expect to find in a restaurant ad from 70-something years ago. There is the notion that emphasis on speed is a recent phenomenon. Actually it isn't: "Fast" and "quick" can be found in New England eatery ads as far back as the wee years of this century.

The Quick Service Cafe appears to have been started by Morrill "Ham" Greenleaf around 1917. It was then operated by one James C. Adams for a brief period in the early 1920s before reverting back to Ham Greenleaf, who ran the restaurant as Greenleaf's Cafe until the mid-1930s. He then moved operations diagonally across the street to the corner of Main and Whitman streets, where he operated a lunchroom until circa 1950.

Ham, who is recalled around town as a jovial, happy-go-lucky sort, passed away in 1968. His - and James C. Clark's - for-mer cafe at 209 Main is now occupied by the Computer Connection (which, due to renumbering, is now 249 Main).

Romar Bowling Lanes
Boothbay Harbor

It almost appears to be a stock-ade. Or a large log cabin. But it is neither. It is the rather funky Romar Bowling Lanes. Romar was opened by Charles <u>Rowe</u> and his brother-in-law Leslie <u>Marr</u> in 1946. Rowe, a Massachusetts native who moved to Maine at age five and graduated from Boothbay Harbor High School in 1933, had been in the bowling business in Boothbay Harbor as proprietor of Robin-son's Lanes. When Robinson's burned down in 1945, he looked around and discovered his own family's property on Bridge Street. A former livery stable, the building was being rented out for stores. But as Rowe recounts: "Stores weren't renting too well in those days, so we moved the alleys up here."

Charles Rowe became sole proprietor in 1956 and the eight-alley lanes have been his baby ever since. Now 78, he looks back on a business that has basically been very good to him. When I visited with him in July 1994, however, he was in the midst of the worst year he'd ever had. He blamed it on "the economy" plus the fact that sections of Boothbay Harbor were torn up for a new sewer line. But he remains optimistic... and prays for rain. "On rainy days and foggy days this place is packed," he beams.

Photo, July 1994. Formerly open year-around, Charles Rowe switched to summer-only in 1984. With Boothbay Harbor's tourist influx being what it is, Charles gets a lot of people "from away" who have never before seen candlepin bowling. But once they try it most of them like it: "Especially the kids. It's much easier for them, with the small ball."

Photo, July 1994. Vern Lewis, 44, and his son, Justin, 10, of Edgecomb, Maine were enjoying Romar's the day I was there. Justin summed up candlepin's allure very simply and very nicely: "It's fun: trying to knock down all the pins."

Ross's Ice Cream
Lewiston

Mention Ross's Ice Cream to most any oldtimer around Lewiston/Auburn and you're almost certain to be rewarded with a big smile. "The best ice cream I ever had," extols 74-year old Bill Rogers of Auburn. "It was really something: his ice cream was better than anything I ever tasted," seconds his wife, Connie. "It was *the* place to go for a cone on a Sunday afternoon," reminisces lifelong Lewistonite Kay Dockman, also 74, while 93-year old Robert Wade still recalls the size of a Ross's cone. "Very liberal helpings," is how he phrases it.

George E. Ross was born in Alexandria, Virginia in 1875. A black, he came to Lewiston to study for the ministry at Bates. While at Bates, from which he received a B.A. degree in 1904, George began making and selling ice cream to assist with expenses. It was something of a second nature for him: as a youngster he'd helped his father make ice cream for the family store in Alexandria.

Deciding that there was little financial reward in the ministry, and that he didn't really like law after studying it for four months in New York City, George returned to Lewiston and again took up the ice cream business. It was meant to be temporary, but proved to be so satisfying that it became his life's calling. It was a good choice. George clearly loved what he did. He was known to break into song while serving customers and, again in the words of Bill Rogers, had "the greatest disposition in the world."

George A. Ross died in June, 1943. His wife Pearl kept the business going for a time, but it wasn't the same. Ross's Ice Cream needed a George A. Ross.

Ross's former shop at 56 Elm Street - where he made and sold his ice cream of renown - is now a two-family private residence.

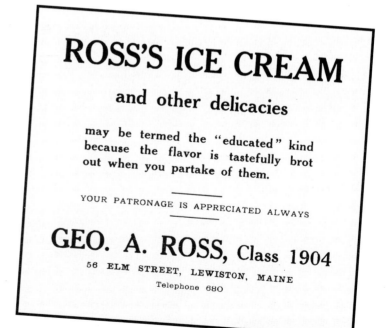

ROSS'S ICE CREAM
and other delicacies

may be termed the "educated" kind because the flavor is tastefully brot out when you partake of them.

YOUR PATRONAGE IS APPRECIATED ALWAYS

GEO. A. ROSS, Class 1904
56 ELM STREET, LEWISTON, MAINE
Telephone 680

Ad, *The Bates Student* newspaper, March 1919. George A. Ross prided himself on his memory... especially when it came to his alma mater, Bates. It is said that if he could not remember the name of a returning alumnus, that alumnus got his ice cream free. Few got free ice cream.

Roy Mack Beverages
Waldoboro

It took a man from Indiana to add Waldoboro to the hefty list of Maine towns that once had their own bottling works. That man was Roy Mack, and he hailed from Hillsdale, Indiana. What brought him to Maine is unknown, but it is known that he started bottling in 1916 when he was 41 years old. Never a big operator, Mack nevertheless turned out a full contingent of flavors, 14 or 15 in total.

Roy Mack died in 1939. His wife Audrey ran the firm for a few years, then sold to Arnold Levensale, a Waldoboro native and an employee. Arnold kept the flavor count up, even trying new ones. Bill Wellman, 58, recalls Roy Mack chocolate soda circa 1946. "It was sweet; tasted like chocolate milk," he says. Other flavors included strawberry, raspberry, root beer, orange, grape, sarsaparilla, lemon & lime, and, of course, ginger ale. All were made with water from a natural spring 300 feet up the hill in back of the plant. The bottling works' last owner was Berton Scott, a Bath and Waldoboro native who was Arnold's nephew and who had worked at the bottling company during the summer. He purchased the operation, still named Roy Mack, in 1957. Two years later, in a 1959 newspaper interview, he hit the nail on the head re being a small bottler: "In this business you have to be a jack of all trades. You must be a bookkeeper, salesman, electrician, machinist, and truck mechanic. It is rugged and the competition is highly competitive."

Bertie solved part of the competition problem in 1962: he bought out Clark Beverages (q.v.) in nearby Newcastle, eventually transferring operations there as it was a newer and larger facility.

Berton Scott died in 1976, age 50. With him died the business. Berton's wife Eleanor, now living in South Portland, sums up her husband's two decades in the soda business fairly succinctly: "It was a small mom and pop business. It was seasonal. It was a good business. We enjoyed it."

The former Roy Mack plant on Friendship Street in Waldoboro is now occupied by Mike's Outboard Service. If he's not too busy, ask proprietor Mike Lailer to show you around. Note especially that the entire building is slanted: a throwback to the time when gravity feed played an important role in "the modern plant."

Courtesy of Elwin Hussey, Windsor

Standing tall in this wonderful 1936 photo of the original Hussey's General Store in Windsor are the store's founders, Mildred Hussey and Harland Hussey... and a Roy Mack soda "machine," too. Through the years Roy Mack bottled O-So-Grape, Moxie, Orange Crush, and the company's own Old Jamaica flavors. Hussey's sold them all.

The Sail Inn
Prospect

Both postcards courtesy of Eddie and Vera Dyer, Prospect

A view that is spectacular. Plus, per proprietor Eddie Dyer, "The best fried clams in Maine... bar none." That's the Sail Inn.

Eddie, 66, is a native of Beverly, Massachusetts, where he worked all through high school in a local diner. "That's how I got interested in the restaurant business," he says. He had an aunt who lived in Stockton Springs. One day she mentioned to him that the Sail Inn was for sale. That was 1946 and Eddie was only 16. Still, he knew his heart. He wanted to own the restaurant and, with his parents' consent and financial help, he did. He paid, as he recalls, "$1,100 or $1,200."

The original Sail Inn - the one Eddie bought and the one pictured here - was located about 200 feet closer to the Waldo-Hancock Bridge than the present-day version. It had roots that went back to circa 1932, was initially owned by a man named Henry Sargent, and was, at one time or another, a gas station, a schoolhouse, a private residence, and, of course, a restaurant. For a time it was known as the Sail In and Anchor.

When Eddie took over, the Sail Inn was thought of more as a bar than a restaurant. Bucksport was dry and his was the only place between Winterport, Ellsworth, and Belfast where people could buy a beer. And people did buy a beer! Eddie laughs as he remembers the restaurant's former "Sail in... stagger out" reputation.

In 1968 Eddie and his wife Vera (they were married in 1949) tore down the old Sail Inn and built the present one. They wanted a bigger place.

Nowadays the Sail Inn is run as much by Eddie and Vera's sons, Bobby and Paul, as it is by Eddie and Vera themselves. And its beer sales are miniscule. Fresh seafood, steaks and chops, and, of course, fried clams and the view: that's the ticket at today's Sail Inn.

SAIL INN AT WALDO-HANCOCK BRIDGE   G38

Postcard view, circa 1956

St. Croix Valley Drive-In Theatre
Baring

"For Sale," the sign reads. It is tiny in comparison to the drive-in theatre screen that stands nearby... yet it looms much, much larger in importance. The St. Croix Valley Drive-In, one of the six remaining operational drive-ins in the state, is for sale. And to make matters worse, it's not really the theatre that's for sale. It's only the land.

But let's back up. To 1954. That's the year the St. Croix Valley Drive-In opened. The original owners were local businessmen Allie Nason and K.J. "Doc" Thomas. Within the year they were joined by K.J.'s son, Kenneth Smith "Smitty" Thomas. "They wanted some young blood," jests the now 66- year old Smitty.

"It was a big deal when it opened," Smitty recounts. Westerns and musicals were the

favorites. So was the food. A lot of people would come more to eat, both Smitty and his son, 35-year old Ken Thomas, recall proudly. Homemade French fries were the biggest hit, but the drive-in's hot dynamites - spicy meatball sandwiches made especially for the 4th of July - satisfied many a taste bud, too. Smitty became sole proprietor in 1962-1963, and both owned and operated the theatre until 1976. Then, tired of the pressure of running the drive-in and a newer venture, the International Motel, Smitty sold the theatre.

The new owner was then 39-year old Rich Bernard. Rich, a native of Caribou, was a teacher who was tired of teaching. The result: he got into show business. His first venture, with his two brothers, was the Braden Theatre in Presque Isle. The second was the St. Croix Valley. Rich bought the drive-in in late fall of 1976, so he had to wait until spring 1977 for his Grand Opening. And it did turn out to be grand, although in a rather roundabout way: it was an April day and was gorgeous at 3:00 PM and Rich decided this was to

Courtesy of Smitty Thomas, Calais

Photo, circa 1965. Smitty's proud that when the St. Croix Valley opened in 1954 it possessed the second largest drive-in screen - 58 feet high by 90 feet wide - in the state. Only the Portland Drive-In in Scarborough had a screen with more square footage.

118

Photo, 1985. In the spring of 1985 the St. Croix Valley's huge original wooden screen blew down during a bad windstorm. During the period of time it took to get a new screen in place Rich had some fun: he put *"Gone With The Wind"* on the marquee.

Courtesy of Lucille and Rich Bernard, Calais

area's drive-in fans - is that there is no buyer. If that's the case, Rich says, then he and Lucille will probably keep the St. Croix Valley alive and running. When I told Rich and Lucille that I, at least, thought their not being able to sell beat the heck out of their being able to sell, they smiled and said they thought that might be the case.

Photo, August 1994. In the many years he's owned the St. Croix Valley Drive-In, one movie stands out in Rich's mind. It's *Coal Miner's Daughter*, the 1980 Loretta Lynn biopic starring Sissy Spacek. "It was incredible," he recalls very vividly. "It was one of those pictures that brought people out of the woodwork."

be the day. Mother Nature, however, had other plans in mind. By 7:00 PM it was "snowing to beat hell." Rich was all set to call the whole thing off... until he noticed that cars - lots of cars - were beginning to line up for the show, snow or no snow. "If they're crazy enough to watch a movie in this snowstorm, I'm crazy enough to show it," declared Rich. And he did.

Today, almost two decades later, Rich will readily admit that buying the drive-in was the best thing he ever did. It enabled him to become his own boss and "make a lot of money." He also says that "Business is good as far

as drive-ins go." Still, he has the theatre site up for sale. There are two reasons why. First, he finds it "next to impossible" to find people who'll work weekends. Second, Rich now also owns the only other theatre in the area, the State, in Calais. He and his wife Lucille have decided they'd rather concentrate their energies on the State. Consequently, they put the drive-in on the market in early summer 1994. And, since Rich doesn't want to sell the St. Croix Valley to someone and then try to put that someone out of business, it's being sold with a deed restriction that there can be no drive-in theatre. Bummer. The only hope - for the

Sesme Car Hop
Caribou

"They said I was crazy, the craziest man in Caribou, to build out there," laughs Ron Smith. Ron, now 60, was reflecting back to when he was 20 and he did, indeed, have a wild and quite possibly crazy idea. The idea was a restaurant with all carhop services...the first curb service restaurant in Caribou. It was to be modeled on a very similar restaurant that Ron had seen in Hartford, Connecticut. In fact it was not only to be modeled after it...it was, for all intents and purposes, to be named after it. The restaurant in Hartford was named Sesame. Ron named his Sesme.

The Sesme Car Hop - much of it built by Ron himself - opened on July 4, 1956. It was a smash

Ad, 1967

Courtesy of Hali Anderson-Milton, South Portland

Photo, 1967. Left to right, carhops Kathy Quimby, Brenda Randolph, Linda Carrier, Carol Hackett, Laura Getchell. Laura - now Laura Violette - still recalls that being a Sesme Car Hop carhop was fun. And that the Sesme was the place to be: "Everybody pulled in, everybody passed through...whether they ordered anything or not."

Courtesy of Linda Violette, Caribou

success from the very start. Hamburgers, chicken and seafood baskets, frosted root beer: all seemed to fly out of the kitchen and into the stomachs of customer after customer...many of whom came from nearby Loring Air Force Base. In was the base, in fact, that was the catalyst for the restaurant. "I could envision it near the base," Ron still recalls vividly.

Ron ran the Car Hop for 19 seasons - April to October - and then decided enough was enough. He saw McDonald's and Burger King coming in. Plus he

was offered a golden opportunity with Aroostook County Federal Savings & Loan. That was 1975. Today, 20 years later, Ron's brainchild still at least partially exists. It serves as the framework for a local restaurant and hotspot named Yusef's/Priority #1 Entertainment Center. And "out there": the stretch of open land northeast of town where people thought Ron especially crazy to locate his dream? It's now "the strip," with Burger King, Pizza Hut, et al. I know that I, at least, would much prefer the Car Hop still serving up its meals. Open Sesme.

Shaw's Ridge Farm
Sanford

The Shaw family has been making ice cream at Shaw's Ridge Farm since Franklin Delano Roosevelt was in his first term as president. If FDR had dropped by, however, he would've had to look hard to find the ice cream: in those days Shaw's Ridge Farm was a full-line dairy, with milk, cream, and eggs the mainstays of the business. And that business came very largely via trucks that delivered door-to-door.

Well, times have changed. Shaw's Ridge is now 100% on-premises sales. And ice cream is king. What happened, 46-year old Richard Shaw will tell you, is that small dairies simply could not compete with the big guys.

Shaw's Ridge sold out to Oakhurst in 1973-1974. All but the ice cream side of the business. They kept that.

And Richard - a seventh-generation Shaw at Shaw's Ridge - is glad of it. First, there's the ice cream itself. "I have a two cone a day addiction," he smiles. But mostly Richard likes being proprietor of a place that people enjoy coming to. "A fun place," he phrases it. Part of the fun is, of course, the ice cream. "A good product and a lot of product for the money," as Richard characterizes it. But the real key may be the Ice Cream Room building - a handsome stone structure that goes back to the 1920s and used to be the milk processing plant - and the grounds. Richard

is real proud of the grounds. All in all, Shaw's Ridge Farm is a York County mecca. "It's an institution," to quote Richard one last time. "I think I'd have to move if I ever closed the Ice Cream Room down."

Photo, June 1994. Another very satisfied customer...who just happens to be my wife, Catherine. C and I enjoyed a number of flavors the day we visited Shaw's Ridge Farm, including one with "a story." It seems an employee in the early 1990s suggested a recipe for a special blend, and then suggested it be called Suffering Succotash. And so it was...until Warner Brothers somehow got wind of the happenings in Sanford and made it clear that "Suffering Succotash" was the trademark of Sylvester the Cat, and that Sylvester the Cat was Warner Brothers' - not Shaw's Ridge Farms' - property. The special blend is now called Chocolate Thunder.

Photo, June 1994. Located on Route 224, Shaw's Ridge Farm is open from Mother's Day to Columbus Day. Cones are the lion's share of the business. And vanilla is still the top seller...with chocolate and coffee not far behind.

Shorette's Diner
Lincoln

Shorette's. It sounds like a 1950's vocal group. Instead it was a 1950's diner...named after a man named Shorette.

Charlie Shorette came to Lincoln, from Mattawamkeag, circa 1950. He'd sighted a prime location for a restaurant. The location was at the corner of Fleming Street and West Broadway/Route 2. In those pre-interstate days everyone going from Bangor to Houlton or vice versa rolled right by the location. The only problem was that there was an 1826 house occupying it. Charlie solved that by buying the house and property, moving the house, and then constructing his restaurant.

Shorette's, which operated from 1950 to 1958, is well remembered in Lincoln. "It was a nice place... a good place for coffee... everybody went there," recalls 80-year old Charlotte

Matchbook cover, circa 1955

Ridley. Shirley Potter, 62, remembers Charlie Shorette as "a good cook" and his restaurant as "a place you could depend on: it was consistently good." And 64-year old Avilda McLaughlin especially recalls Shorette's. She should: she worked there. Avilda recollects that Shorette's served "good, complete meals...just like the big restaurants in Bangor;" that Charlie had a strict dress code with white always the order of the day; and that Charlie was proud that Shorette's had its own pastry chef. She also recalls Charlie as a good-natured, "happy go lucky" sort. Avilda laughs when she thinks back to when this good nature was tested. To the limit. It seems that one of Charlie's waitresses possessed an extremely devilish sense of humor. "She was an imp," chuckles Avilda. Well, one night a couple from away came in at a time

when the smell from the local paper mill was especially strong. "What is that awful odor?," asked the couple. "Oh," replied the waitress, "that's the baked beans cooking in the kitchen. And", she continued, "don't they smell lovely?" She had them hooked. They both ordered baked beans. The only problem, of course, was that there were no baked beans on Shorette's menu. When the waitress told Charlie, he lived up to his good-natured reputation. "He almost died laughing," Avilda herself laughs so hard she can barely finish the story. "Then he sent someone to the store for canned baked beans on the double."

Charlie Shorette closed his restaurant in 1958. Since then it's been Taylor's Diner, and Olivieri's. Now, much remodeled, it's the Timber House Restaurant. Baked beans are served on Saturdays.

Skowhegan Drive-In
Skowhegan

Doug Corson well recalls the early days of the Skowhegan Drive-in: it was so popular that people would pay just to be able to park in the rear of the lot, hoping they'd be able to hear at least some sound from other peoples' speakers. "We were definitely filled to capacity in those days," he laughs.

Doug has been with the theatre almost as long as it's been in existence. The drive-in opened in June of 1953. Doug began working there in 1956, while still a student at Skowhegan High. The original owners were Lockwood and Gordon Enterprises, head-quartered in Boston. In 1969 they sold to SBD Management Corp., which in turn sold to Encor Skowhegan Theatre Corp., owned by Doug, in 1985.

Doug has definitely enjoyed his almost 40 years at the drive-in. And he's still enjoying it. He especially likes the customers... "the people I've had a chance to meet." Moreover, he reports that business is up - just slightly, but still up - these past three seasons. And based on that, he ventured that "the prognosis for the the-atre is reasonably good." And that's very good.

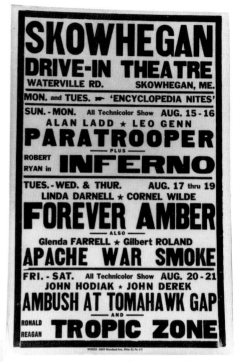

Advertising poster from 1953, the theatre's inaugural year. The drive-in is located on East Front Street/Route 2, and is open from early May to mid-September.

Photo, July 1994. *Jurassic Park* is the Skowhegan Drive-In's all-time box office success story, playing to crowds in both 1993 and 1994.

Photo, July 1994. In addition to standard drive-in fare, Doug also sells T-shirts at his concession stand. My favorite reads: "Drive-Ins Forever."

State Theatre
Bridgton

No, Bridgton wasn't the Great White Way. But it was a two-theatre town for most of Hollywood's golden years. On one side of Main Street was the Mayfair (please see pages 88-89); on the other, the State. The State was the new kid, built by local real estate magnate Eugene Tenney in 1935-1936. Clarence "Dutch" Millet was longtime manager.

"It was modern, with carpeting and seats that were comfortable," are the words 51-year old Pat Mitchell uses to describe the State. Forty-six year old Elaine Rioux recalls it as "good-sized and roomy," while 75-year old Henry Shorey proclaims the the-

atre to have been "excellent for a town its size."

The State's presence, though, was not to be as long and prosperous as it might've been. Heavy snow accumulated on the theatre's roof during the winter of 1968-1969. Management knew it might prove fatal, but there was too

much danger involved in attempting to remove it.

So they cordoned off the area...and waited. "It was like a death watch," recalls Elaine.

The end came in March, 1969. The theatre's underpinning gave way. Damage was so extensive that what remained was razed. On the State's former site, at the corner of Main and Elm Streets, there is today a restaurant named 78 Main street.

State Theatre
Farmington

John Moore is a young guy who respects old things. And that's good...because John, 29, operates a theatre that's hardly new. What is now the State Theatre began as the Broadway Theatre in February of 1924. At the time *The Franklin Journal* heralded it as "the finest theatre of its size in New England." Perhaps so, but its owner, E.G. Pollard, was simply not able to compete with his across-the-street rival, the Music Hall, and its proprietor, Erland Hardy. The result was that Hardy bought out the Broadway circa 1925 and moved his operations there. (The former Music Hall, incidentally, is now home to Reny's: walk in, head directly upstairs, and be prepared to be impressed!).

The theatre's name was changed to the State in October 1935. Several changes in proprietorship later, it ended up being owned by Hoyt's, the Boston-

Postcard view, circa 1940. The State may have been modern, but it was not air conditioned. Henry Shorey recalls the tale of the usher who was asked "Where's the coolest spot?" by a summer person one especially hot and sticky evening. "Outside." he replied...only to discover his boss had overheard him. He was, alas, fired on the spot.

Ad, September 1935

Ad, September 1936

The State opened as the Broadway in 1924; became the State on Columbus Day, 1935.

sion, John has done a ton to transform the State into a Franklin County showplace. He's put in new seats, Dolby Sound, air conditioning, and turned it into a twin (with plans to buy the upstairs floor and add two more screens). He's also repainted the interior: what used to be "Pepto-Bismol pink" is now what John calls "State Theatre blue and cream." But there remains a nice blend of the old, too. Look for the original tin roof and clock in the lobby; original floors and wallparameter detail in the auditoriums.

Ed. Note: As *More Good Old Maine* was going to press I unfortunately learned from John that, due to not-being-able-to-expand problems, he had decided to close the State at the end of August 1995 and create a new theatre complex in Farmington. The fate of the State is unknown.

based cinema giant: they'd bought a string of theatres and the State was one of them. John, who'd been in the movie business since his sophomore year at Colby and was then manager of the State, was given the opportunity to lease it. He accepted, taking over as of October 30, 1987. How did he feel? "Pretty scared," he'll admit. "I was 23 years old and completely broke." Since his day of deci-

Photo of artwork above the theatre's entrance at 51 Broadway, June 1994. John commissioned Kingfield sign painter Mike Monahan to enhance the State's entrance. That's exactly what Mike did: it's quite gorgeous.

The State as located on the first floor of the majestic Odd Fellows' building in this June 1994 photo.

125

State Theatre
Presque Isle

Many's the Maine town that has had a "State Theatre." Presque Isle has had two. The first opened in what had been the Perry Theatre on Main Street on October 10, 1935. The theatre's Gala Premiere witnessed a second premiere as well: on the screen was *The Farmer Takes A Wife*, featuring Henry Fonda in his very first Hollywood role. State number one delighted Presque Isle moviegoers for a decade before it was destroyed by fire in late January 1945.

The second coming of the State took place in August 1946.

Owned by J.W. Bridgham & Sons of Dover, New Hamphshire - who had also operated the original State - the new State was located around the corner from its predecessor. Hailed as "Beautiful" and "Comfortable" and "One of the state's finest," the State opened with Barbara Stanwyck, Van Heflin, and Elizabeth Scott in *The Strange Love Of Martha Ivers*, and played topflight fare until it was closed in May 1961. The building was subsequently torn down. Its former site at 203 State Street is today occupied by a parking lot.

Courtesy of Northeast Historic Film, Bucksport

STATE STREET, PRESQUE ISLE, MAINE   A340

Postcard view, circa 1950. All the buildings in this view still stand today except, alas, for the State. Worthy of note is the 1918 Crown Travel building, just to the left of the theatre's site. It can almost be called adorable.

State Theatre
Portland

Kelly Graves spent a year of college in Oklahoma in 1983-84... and hated it. Back home in Michigan she found a map of the USA, closed her eyes, and placed her finger down. "Wherever it lands, that's where I'll move," she vowed. Her finger landed on Portland.

I asked Kelly what would have happened had her finger landed on Jackson, Mississippi. She laughed and said "I guess I'd have gone there." Well, Jackson's loss is Portland's gain: after graduating from USM and paying her dues as a waitress and later banquet manager, Kelly now finds herself co-custodian of one of Maine's pop culture masterpieces.

When it opened in November 1929 the State was billed as "The Wonder Theatre." It was a sobriquet well deserved. Superlatives flowed like promises during an election year: "Embodies every device known to modern science;" "A treasure house of beauty;" "The Show Place of Maine;" "Designed and decorated in the style of old Spain." The State had it all: bronze doors, tapestry galore, wrought iron balustrades, Spanish tile floors, wall and ceiling murals, etc. "Richness of color in lobby, foyer and auditorium is toned into one harmonious rainbow," ran one especially laudatory Grand Opening phrase.

STATE BUILDING, PORTLAND, MAINE   OA4147

Courtesy of Maine Historic Preservation Commission, Augusta

Nor was the theatre's graciousness confined to its architectural majesty. Eighteen attendants - attired in "military uniforms of French Blue" - were on hand to serve patrons "with military snap and precision," to "accept instead of taking your tickets," and to "show you to your seats in the manner of an almost forgotten age of chivalry." It was also comforting to know that the State had its own independent power system, the only theatre so equipped in all of New England. The world outside might be coming to an end, but inside the State the show would go on.

And the show did go on. For just over 60 years. It may not have always been the show origi-

nally intended - the State was a porn house from 1969 until its closing on January 1, 1990 - but it was a show. Maine's "Wonder Theatre" then sat empty and unused, an all-too-poignant example of the decline and fall of the downtown movie palace. There was talk of it being transformed into a supper club/theatre. Or a performing arts center. Or a concert hall. But it was all talk until the building's owners, Nick and Lola Kampf, along with Russell Turner and a cast of volunteers, moved in 1993 and gave rebirth. Part of the birthing team was Kelly, 29, and her husband, Stephen Bailey, 39. Now they are, basically, *the* team. Along with partner Kim Magid, they formed Perfect

Pitch, Inc. and took over control of the theatre in August, 1994.

When I spoke with Kelly in January 1995 she was upbeat but admitted the State needed more "community support"... which translates to more packed houses. Not just when a Bob Dylan or a Los Lobos adorns the stage, but for other shows as well. "People looking in think we're very successful and that we must be printing money, but the costs of running (the theatre) and the upkeep," explains Kelly, "are far larger than anyone can imagine." Kelly also admits that the theatre, as beautiful as it is, is not restored to its original grandeur. She and Stephen would like it to be, however, and one suspects, in talking with her, that it eventually will be. "Being," Kelly concludes, "in this building and walking through it every day and looking at the beauty and feeling the history: it's intoxicating."

Photo, January 1995. From Bob Dylan to Bo Diddley to the Maine State Ballet to *Casablanca* on a big, big screen: the reborn State could be called a one-stop entertainment palace.

Photos, both November 1994. "Dramatic" is the word that I think best describes the Stonington Opera House. There it stands, majestically, on Russ's Hill. And if it's not the tallest structure in Stonington, it sure looks it... the Skyscraper of Stonington. It attained National Historic status in 1991.

Stonington Opera House
Stonington

The Stonington Opera House was constructed in 1912 on the same site as its predecessor, the Music Hall, which burned to the ground in 1910. Dr. B. Lake Noyes and D. Jewett Noyes were the major proprietors, and they kept the citizenry well entertained with a hearty diet of silent movies and travelling vaudeville troupes. As with most small town theatres, however, the Opera House was more. It was the town's gathering place, where town meetings and graduations were held. And into the 1930s it was home to Stonington High's basketball team... Stonington High's *championship* basketball team, local historians Clayton Gross and Genice Welcome both make perfectly clear!

Dr. Lewis Tewksbury bought the Opera House in 1928 and owned it through 1953. In the ensuing years a number of owners have struggled with the operation of a built-in-1912 theatre in a television and VCR era. Since 1979 Mike Connors has been the theatre's owner and guiding force. Mike, 48, is a native New Yorker, a successful antiques dealer and teacher, and a man who respects old things. He unabashedly admits to having bought the theatre to "try to save it." And he's poured considerable money into doing just that. Movies were shown - summers only - through 1992. That's the year Stonington put in a new sewer system... and between the blasting and the digging, per town manager Roger Stone, "It just about closed the town down." Now Mike's goal is to get the Opera House rolling again... so that, in his own words, "it may again become a community gathering spot."

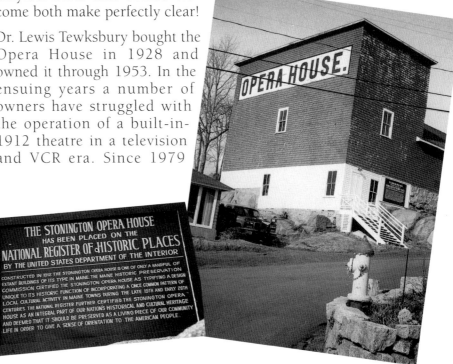

128

Strand Theatre
Portland

The Strand's roots stretch back to a roller-skating rink named Convention Hall, which was remodeled and reopened as the Big Nickel Theatre in April 1911. With 1,500 seats, the Big Nickel ("Biggest Show at Littlest Price") could claim to be the largest movie house in New England. In early 1915, management decided that such a worthy enterprise deserved a more worthy name. They selected "Strand," presumably inspired by New York City's palatial movie house of the same name.

In 1917 management went one step further. They spent the then astronomical sum of $180,000 to completely remodel the theatre. The interior was gutted and, in a process that took eight months, was created anew. It was worth the wait: when reopened in June 1918 the new Strand could rightly be heralded as "The Finest, Safest, and Most Modern Playhouse in New England."

The 1920s were probably the crowning years for the Strand. The theatre featured Leo LeSeur - "The Leading Theatre Organist In The Country" - on the Strand's Grand Organ, and the Strand Symphony Orchestra, a 20-piece aggregation headed by Arthur F. Kendall. For three shows a day the stage would be lighted, and the orchestra would play. "Many in the audience," wrote Harold Boyle in a 1981 *Evening Express* story, "came to hear the orchestra instead of watching the two and three-reel movies." One of these

was a young Rudy Vallee, who worked as an usher at the Strand from 1918 to 1920, and who would later call Arthur F. Kendall his idol.

The Strand and its majesty - "There was marble and chandeliers and gilt brocade and satin and velvet," once wrote an *Evening Express* reporter - delighted audiences through the thirties and forties and fifties. By the 1960s, though, TV and changing entertainment tastes caught up with the "Most Modern Playhouse in New England." It closed in 1963, and was demolished in 1970. Its facade, the Strand Building (561-571 Congress Street), however, still stands, today occupied by a variety of shops and businesses.

Courtesy of Sullivan Photo, Portland.

Photo, December 1962. The marquee of the Strand proclaiming what would be its last Christmas show.

Temple Theatre
Houlton

The year was 1919. Babe Ruth was still with the Red Sox. Woodrow Wilson was in the White House. Mary Pickford was America's Sweetheart. And the Temple Theatre opened in May. At the start the theatre was leased to G. Beecher Churchill, Houlton's Mr. Movie Mogul: at one time or another he controlled the Dream Theatre and Society Hall as well as the Tem-

ple. But the Temple was almost certainly his favorite. How could it not have been? After all, it cost the then rather magnificent sum of $80,000 to construct the theatre building. And the building presented quite an impressive sight. It was three stories high with the theatre on floor number one, offices on floor number two, and a Masonic Temple on floor number three. It was the latter, of course, that gave the theatre its name.

The Babe was traded to the Yankees in 1920. Woodrow Wilson exited the White House in 1921. Mary Pickford made her last movie in 1933. But, a full 75 years after its opening, the Temple Theatre is still wowing Houlton audiences. Actually, "wowing" might be too strong a word. When I interviewed manager Herb Hockenhull in September of 1994 he characterized business as "all right." As he said: "If you've got something

Postcard view, circa 1943. Houlton was humming when they took this shot! The Houlton Theatre, owned by the same company, was the Temple's neighbor from 1941 until it was closed in 1960.

they want to see, then they'll come. If not, they won't." The biggest draw in Herb's tenure at the Temple - which goes back to 1978 - is *Grease*. "I can remember that they came in and just about bowled over the ticket booth - and the lady in it - to get in to see that one," laughs Herb. *Beverly Hills Cop*, *E.T.*, and *Gremlins* have all played big at the Temple as well.

When I asked Herb, who's 48 and a native of Fort Fairfield, about the Temple's amazing longevity, he had a good answer. He attributes it to the fact that the theatre has never been the only business in the building. There are still offices on the second floor and the Masons still hold sway on the third. And, as

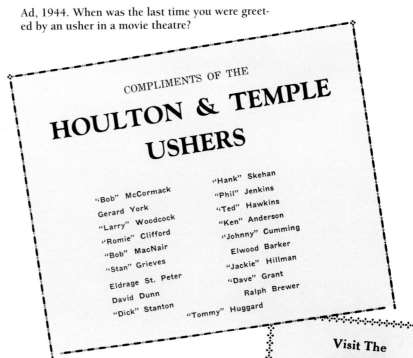

Photo, September 1994. The Temple Theatre Building: still handsome today.

it's always been, the Masons own the building, leasing out the theatre. (It presently is leased to an outfit in Falmouth called Listak Sales and Service). The fact that Houlton has not been "blessed" with a multi-screen complex is obviously a major factor, too. In any event, let us hope that the Temple just keeps on rolling along. It was twinned in 1980, and much of the theatre's original detail has been removed or covered over. But there are stained glass windows in Herb's office, a nifty old Manley popcorn machine, and, my favorite, a marvelous Brandt Junior Automatic Cashier - a change maker - that's been in use so long that there's a sizable hole worn in the change tray. "It's a hole," as a

1993 *Houlton Pioneer Times* article so majestically phrased it, "from the rivers of change which have flowed through."

Photo, circa 1942. "I always told him he was missing a hubcap," Albert Giberson laughs all these years later.

And Albert was right: notice Arthur's back tire.

Courtesy of the A-1 Diner and the Gibersons, Gardiner.

A.E. Thompson
Gardiner

Arthur E. Thompson was a gutsy guy. At age ten or so he lost both an arm and an eye when accidentally hit by a blast from his brother's shotgun. Arthur could have sat around and felt sorry for himself. Instead he became a farmhand in his hometown of Brooks, Maine. His real success, however, came after he moved to Gardiner, circa 1936, and began a home delivery service. Longtime friend and neighbor Albert Giberson recalls Thompson as "always on the road." He had a route that took him as far afield as Lewiston, Skowhegan, Belfast, and Brunswick. Arthur's wife, Daisy, pitched in, too. "She was always cooking," remembers Albert.

Hulled corn, horseradish, and sauerkraut were Arthur and Daisy's specialties. "They were their own productions," reminisces Albert's wife Elizabeth, explaining that Arthur would also buy baked and other goods along his route... and then sell them at a markup. "He was a sharp trader," Elizabeth smiles.

For a man with one arm, Arthur kept it busy. The Gibersons recall that "He was always polishing and waxing" his truck and his several cars. And he'd shovel out his neighbors during snowstorms.

Arthur Thompson made his hulled corn and his horseradish and his sauerkraut and operated his route until circa 1950. He then "retired"

to various jobs at Gardiner Shoe Company. He died in Gardiner at age 87 in 1990.

20th Century Lanes
Biddeford

When it first opened in September of 1938, 20th Century Lanes was lauded as "the first streamlined alleys" in the State of Maine. "All the latest ideas and improvements have been worked in and the room itself is a picture of beauty," rang out the *Biddeford Daily Journal*.

The 20th Century was the brainchild of then 33-year old Sofokli "Mike" Anton. It's not surprising: bowling alleys were in his blood. His father, Adham Anton, had come to America from Albania in 1905, and after success with a bakery, was persuaded to open a bowling alley in Biddeford in 1923. Called the Pastime, it featured 10 of the finest lanes - candlepin, of course - in southern Maine. Plus, there were billiards, a restaurant, and a huge social/athletic hall. The Pastime was quite the place! It was, as Mike describes it, "the biggest thing in York County; everybody was there."

Then came 1929. The Depression. Times were tough. Mike (himself born in Albania, in 1905) and his wife Edna pitched in to keep the Pastime going. And when Adham died, in 1936, Mike took over... building leagues and helping to introduce women to bowling, too. The result was a boom in business, so much so that Mike decided Biddeford could support another set of candlepin alleys. Since the middle of the century was looming near, he decided to call them 20th Century Lanes.

Since its inception almost six decades ago, the 20th Century has seen it all: changes in ownership, the inroad of ten pins, the decline of downtown. Still, the 20th Century hangs in there. In 1949 Mike sold the alleys to help pay for the construction of Big 20 Lanes in Scarborough (today operated by Mike's son, Chris). Since then Edgar Morin, Nick Gillis, Scott Cochrane, and Frances Beaulieu have all done their thing as proprietors of the lanes. Today's owner is 46-year old Mike Cleary. A Biddeford native, Mike easily recalls his father and himself frequenting 20th Century when he was a youngster. As a result - although he catagorizes his bowling business as "not good" - he is reluctant to kiss candlepins goodbye. Four alleys remain. They get a pretty good workout from Universtiy of New England students on weekends. Then there's Mike's triathlon: three times a year he hosts a triple play of bowling, darts, and pool, with cash prizes for the top three finishers plus a trophy for number one.

Does Mike know that he's the guardian of the last of the old-time upstairs bowling alleys in all of Maine? Yep. Would he and Mike Anton - still wonderfully hale and hearty at age 89 - agree on many things? Probably not. Except, perhaps, that the 20th Century is a pretty unique place.

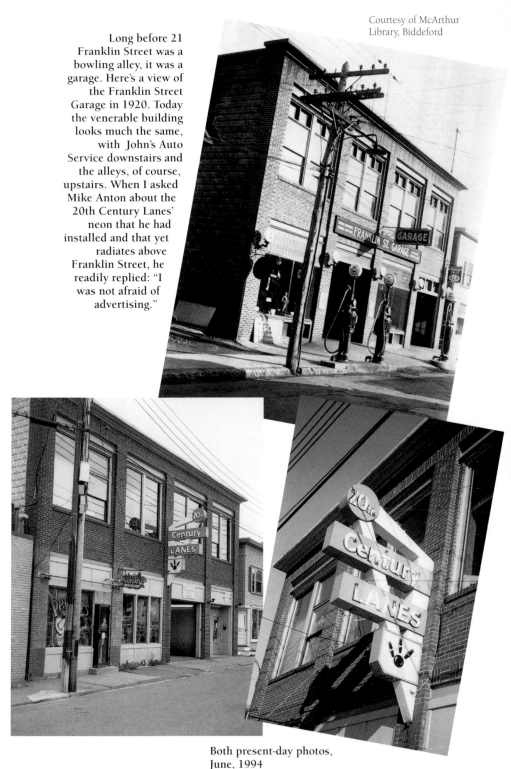

Courtesy of McArthur Library, Biddeford

Long before 21 Franklin Street was a bowling alley, it was a garage. Here's a view of the Franklin Street Garage in 1920. Today the venerable building looks much the same, with John's Auto Service downstairs and the alleys, of course, upstairs. When I asked Mike Anton about the 20th Century Lanes' neon that he had installed and that yet radiates above Franklin Street, he readily replied: "I was not afraid of advertising."

Both present-day photos, June, 1994

Postcard view. In the summer of 1930 the City of Westbrook honored its famous son by naming the area in front of Vallee Pharmacy "Rudy Vallee Square." This view, looking for all the world as if Rudy and/or the crowd were "dubbed in," is most likely from that year.

Courtesy of Maine Historic Preservation Commission, Augusta

Greetings from Rudy Vallee's Home Town, Westbrook, Maine.

Vallee Pharmacy
Westbrook

The most famed name in the history of Westbrook? That's easy. Vallee. Rudy Vallee will, after all, be always and forever inextricably linked to Maine's 11th largest city. But we're here to talk about Rudy's dad, Charles Vallee, and his drug store and soda fountain.

Charles Alphonse Vallee was born in Island Pond, Vermont in 1868. He was educated in the public schools, graduated from Sherbrooke College (in Sherbrooke, Quebec), and became a druggist. He was involved with drug stores in Island Pond and Rumford (Maine) before moving to Westbrook in 1907. There, in early 1908, he purchased the Woodman Pharmacy on the corner of Main and Bridge streets. Established by Charles Woodman in 1869, the Woodman Pharmacy was a fixture in Westbrook. Charles Vallee wasted no time in carrying on that tradition. A June 1908 ad (for the now-named Vallee Pharmacy) announced the "opening of the Soda season," touted such specialties as the banana split, the cherry top, and the marshmallow tip, and assured one and all that "Our Soda is served in sterilized glasses." A 1911 ad billed Vallee's as "The Down-To-Date Drug Store With The Up-To-Date Fountain" and boasted of Westbrook's only Automatic Carbonator... the better to serve soda "that is alive." An early interior photo shows the fountain of the

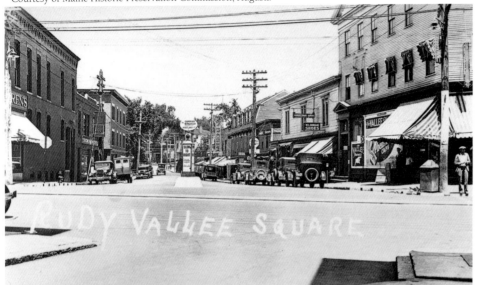

Postcard view, circa 1930. The substantial Vallee Pharmacy building pictured here on the right was destroyed by fire in 1942. But the store lived on in the form of a new 1½-story cement structure that's still there. The tradition of service and "Prices right" lived on also. Westbrook native Betty Tracy, 71, recalls the coffee breaks she and her co-workers enjoyed at Vallee's in the late 1950s: "We only had 15 minutes and they (Vallee's) would always make sure there were a couple of stools waiting for us so we could have our coffee and get back on time." And Henry Gagnon, who's 70 and now owns the structure, remembers that Vallee's ice cream cones had "a little bigger dip" than the other places in town.

Vallee Pharmacy (also known as "The Rexall Store") to be handsome, with a marble-topped counter and a proliferation of signs advertising the likes of college ices, sundaes, Moxie ("Very Healthful") and Goold's Orangeade.

Charles Vallee was a firm believer in advertising. And especially in slogans. During the 1920s he, in fact, had so many slogans he had to take turns using them. My favorite is "Prices right; Goods right. That's all."

After 40 years in the business, Charles Vallee sold his store in 1929. In retirement he travelled extensively, gardened, and occasionally hobnobbed with his famous son on stage. He died in 1949. His store lived longer. Always called the Vallee Pharmacy (The name "Vallee" was, after all, magic. The enterprise, in fact, was often advertised as "Maine's Most Famous Drug

Store."), it was long operated by John Moore and then, after his death in 1945, by his widow, Elizabeth. The store's last owner was Robert Berry of Auburn. It was he who closed it in 1974. Since then the former pharmacy has been used as a shoe store, a pizza parlor, and, since 1991, a tropical fish outlet.

Rudy Vallee (1901-1986)

Born in Vermont, Rudy (real name: Hubert) Vallee grew up in Westbrook, spent a year at UMO, is most closely identified with Maine. With his band, the Connecticut Yankees, the crooner/saxophonist gained national fame via his weekly radio show, broadcast live from the Heigh-Ho Club in New York, 1929-1939. The show ranked second only to Amos and Andy in popularity. And when he married (for the second of four times) in 1931, distraught female fans peppered him with 10,000 "How could you do it?" letters and telegrams.

Song hits included *My Time Is Your Time* (his theme song), *I'm Just a Vagabond Lover, Marie, Good Night, Sweetheart,* plus, of course, the (University of Maine) *Stein Song.* Movies included *The Vagabond Lover* (1929), *The Palm Beach Story* (1942), many others, including *How To Succeed in Show*

Business Without Really Trying (1967). When he died in 1986, *Time* called him "the singing idol of the Depression era," adding: "Before such latterday legends as Bing Crosby, Frank Sinatra and Elvis Presley, there was Vallee."

Sheet music cover, 1929. Although proud of his father, Rudy Vallee had little interest in the pharmacy business. He would later admit, however, that it had its advantages. "Think back to the days when *you* were a youngster," he wrote in 1962. "Wouldn't you have loved to run amuck among nine, count 'em, *nine* different flavors of ice cream?"

Wa-Co Diner
Eastport

You might logically expect that "Wa-Co" is short for <u>Wa</u>shington <u>Co</u>unty. After all, Eastport - the easternmost city in the U.S. - is very much in Washington County. But "Wa-Co" stands, instead, for <u>Wa</u>tts and <u>Co</u>lwell, the last names of the two men most closely identified with the diner.

Eastport legend has it that a portrait photographer by the name of Cecil Greenlaw went to a fair somewhere in the New York /Philadelphia area, fell in love with a lunch cart he saw in operation there, and bought the cart. He then had it hauled to Eastport, where he used it as a photo studio. That was around 1918. Several years later, circa 1921, a man named Grover Boynton purchased

Courtesy of Betty Ferguson, Wa-Co Diner, Eastport

Photo, circa 1922, after the lunch cart that had become a photo studio became a lunch cart again. That's proud proprietor Grover Boynton on the left, friend Winifred Cummings on the right. Diner expert Larry Cultrera of Medford, Massachusetts estimates the cart to be a turn-of-the-century model and manufactured by either C.H. Palmer or T.H. Buckley, both lunch wagon manufacturing kingpins in Worcester, Massachusetts.

it... and converted it back to a lunch cart again. He'd go from sardine factory to sardine factory selling his lunches and coffee. In 1924 the structure changed hands again. The new owners were Nelson Watts and Ralph Colwell, who continued to operate the lunch cart on a travelling basis for their first decade of business. In 1934, however, they decided it was time to settle down. They constructed a permanent structure in Bank Square (Water Street). The Wa-

Co's been there ever since. Elliott Thompson, longtime Wa-Co cook, bought the diner in the early 1960s. It was he who built the present day structure - "The New Wa-Co" - in 1971. Since 1986 the Wa-Co has been owned by Elliott's daughters, Betty (Ferguson) and Patricia (Magoon), and son, Barry. When I spoke with Betty in January of 1995 she said she's proud of her food and of her service. But the highlight of her years at the diner came in

1994. She, Barry, and Patricia decided to throw a birthday party - a year long birthday party! -to celebrate the Wa-Co's 70th. They hung banners, created an array of commerative shirts and hats, and garnered lots of nice publicity. And why not: in a city that's seen the changes Eastport has seen (A 1994 article by writer Joanne O'Grady referred to Eastport as "this city of vacant buildings."), 70 years is, indeed, something of which to be proud.

Photo, August 1994. The Wa-Co (pronounced "Whacko") has been a fixture in downtown Eastport since the days of Dizzy Dean (since 1934, to be precise, the year "01 Diz" was 30-7 and then won two more in the World Series). That's a lot of years and a lot of coffee, hamburgers, sandwiches, pies et al. They're all still popular, naturally, but also big sellers now are beef stew, pea soup, and bread - all homemade, of course. But the biggest seller of all, Betty tells me, is fish and chips. People look forward to having that as a real treat. In fact, Betty tells me that she was recently in Bangor and ran into an old friend from Eastport and the friend took one look at her and almost before she even said "Hello" she said "I can't wait to go down home and have fish and chips at the diner."

Circa 1932
postcard view

Ad, 1928.

Wedgemere
Ogunquit

"Gleason" and "good food" were almost synonymous in Ogunquit in the 1920s and 1930s. Beginning in 1921, George and Marie Gleason owned and operated the much-touted Gleason's Famous Lobster House on Beach Street. Three years later, in 1924, the couple opened a second place...which they named Wedgemere. Located on the Post or State Road - later to become U.S. Route 1 - Wedgemere offered overnight accommodations as well as meals. It's the food that's remembered. "It was a nice place": those are the words that both Charlotte Moody, 65, and Sylvia Hutch-

ins, 78, use to describe Wedgemere. Agatha Coombs, 87, is more generous with her praise: "The food was excellent. It was prepared the way it should be and served right. She (Marie Gleason) knew how to cook!"

George passed away circa 1927. Marie ran things herself until 1938. She then sold to sisters Clara and Mary Richardson, who changed the name to Richardson's Ogunquit Inn. In the late 1960s, Richard Perkins became proprietor, and another name change - to Poor Richard's Pub - was made. Circa 1988 the handsome old structure was demolished. On the site now is Ocean Towers Resort Motel.

Weferling's
Portland/Bangor

From Portland to Bangor to California: such was the career path of John H.F. Weferling. He first appears in Portland in 1894 as proprietor of Weferling's Restaurant at 508 Congress Street. By 1897 he was in partnership with a confectioner named Charles W. Cordes. And by 1898 he was gone. "Moved to Bangor," read the city directory.

In the Lumber City, Weferling set up shop as a caterer at 91 Main Street. But his stay was to be a short one. By 1902 he was gone again, this time to California. John H.F. Weferling was not to be seen around Maine again. His name, though, lived on... thanks to Lewis Hegwein.

Hegwein, a native of New York City, where he was born in 1877, had been employed in restaurants and hotels his entire working life. He began in his father's lunchrooms in New York, and then moved on to various hotels in New York and the south. Bangor beckoned in 1898. Hegwein worked at Weferling's for a year or so before moving on once more, this time to Virginia. Bangor was in his blood, however: in 1902 he returned and purchased Weferling's.

Hegwein retained the Weferling name. It does have a nice lilt to it. Moreover, he continued to

embellish it with the words "Vienna Cafe." And, as one might expect of an Austrian cafe, Hegwein emphasized pastries and confections. Ice cream and ices were also a feature of the house. "Keep cool with Weferling's" may not have been an actual slogan, but it most certainly could have been.

Weferling's Vienna Cafe, always at 91 Main Street, operated until 1911. By all accounts it was one of Bangor's leading eating places. A 1909 article, in fact, credited Lewis Hegwein with having "gained for his establishment a reputation which is second to none." By 1911, however, Hegwein was most likely weary from the responsibility that comes with being sole proprietor of a restaurant. He closed the cafe, and joined forces with local sausage maker Christian Rabenstein in a delicatessen, at 32 Central Street, named Hegwein & Rabenstein. It was to be short-lived: Hegwein moved to Boston in 1913.

The site of Weferling's Vienna Cafe, on the ground floor of a good-looking four story brick building at 91 Main Street, is today occupied by Willey's Karate and Jujitsu.

INDEX

140